SON OF GOD

ANGELA TILBY

INTRODUCED BY

JEREMY BOWEN

Hodder & Stoughton
LONDON SYDNEY AUCKLAND

First published in Great Britain in 2001,
by arrangement with the BBC.

British Library Cataloguing in Publication Data

A record for this book is available from the British Library

ISBN 0 340 78578 0

Typeset by Avon Dataset Ltd, Bidford-on-Avon, Warks

Printed and bound in Great Britain by
Clays Ltd, St Ives plc

Hodder & Stoughton
A Division of Hodder Headline Ltd
338 Euston Road
London NW1 3BH

CONTENTS

INTRODUCTION
BY JEREMY BOWEN

These days, most of us in Britain are not very religious. But the life of Jesus, a man who lived and breathed just like we do, still casts a giant shadow over us. In our television films in the *Son of God* series we explored the world in which Jesus lived. Now this excellent book puts it all down on to the printed page.

I lived in Jerusalem for more than five years. The BBC sent me there to be its Middle East correspondent. To get the job, I had to submit myself to a BBC appointments board, a panel of senior journalists and managers, who asked me searching questions about how I would cover the news in one of the most turbulent parts of the world. The questions reflected the usual preoccupations of educated westerners: we discussed politics, peace and war. But we hardly touched on religion. While outside rain soaked into West London, inside we spent a few minutes groping around the subject of Islamic fundamentalism. Then we cast it aside in favour of issues more congenial to European minds.

A few months later, when for the first time I went on a light and clear Jerusalem morning to the Mount of Olives to look down on the holy city, I started to realise that religion was a little more pervasive there than I or my inquisitors in London had imagined. The Muslim call to prayer was echoing around the domes and the minarets. Religious Jews were praying in their cemetery on the slopes of the Mount of Olives. Christian pilgrims were heading for the Garden of Gethsemane at the foot of the Mount.

Living in Jerusalem helped me to understand that religion is a vital, intimate, sometimes dominating part of modern life in the Holy Land. More than five years in Jerusalem, a city that is sacred to the world's three great monotheistic religions, did not make me into a believer. But it did make me realise that the almost completely secular society I knew in Britain was unusual. Around the world, many hundreds of millions of people do not define themselves by their jobs, or by the football team they support, or by the kind of music they like. Instead, their lives are shaped, directed sometimes, by religion.

When we made the *Son of God* films for BBC1, we set out to recreate the world in which Jesus lived. Before the actors could start work on the dramatic reconstructions of his life, we had to find the latest scholarship to get the history right. In the last decade, new archaeological discoveries have helped us to understand much more about first-century Palestine. Experts took us to the latest digs all around the Holy Land. We filmed the two-thousand-year-old fishing boat that Israeli kibbutzniks discovered in the mud on the shores of the Sea of Galilee, and that has just emerged from a decade and more of restoration. It is likely that Jesus and his followers had a boat that was very similar to this one. We used the latest computer graphics techniques to virtually rebuild the environment Jesus would have known – from the Roman city of Sepphoris, close to Nazareth, to the ancient Jewish temple in Jerusalem. And, what might Jesus have looked like? We commissioned a forensic artist to rebuild a face on the cast of a skull of a first-century man that had been found in a Jewish grave in modern Israel. It wasn't Jesus, of course. But it perhaps gives us the best representation yet of what he might have looked like. Forget those old Bible pictures of a tall, blond-haired, northern European. He was more likely to have been short, intense and dark.

As you will find in this book, there is compelling historical evidence that a man called Jesus lived in Palestine around two thousand years ago. He formulated a series of ideas that were developed by his followers and which still resonate around the world. All that is certain.

And was he really the Son of God? Well, that is not something that can be proved. You either believe it or you don't . . .

JEREMY BOWEN

PREFACE

What can we really know about Jesus of Nazareth, the founder of Christianity and the central figure in the worship and message of the Christian Church? Two thousand years after his death, the answer is that we know a great deal – probably more than has been known about him at any time since he walked the hills of Galilee. For some 400 years his life has been under scrutiny by scholars who have struggled to separate the dogmas about Jesus from the historical facts. Now, at the start of the twenty-first century, at the dawn of a new millennium of the Christian era, the labours of these scholars are bearing fruit.

The sources for what we now know about Jesus are both ancient and recent. The most obvious ancient source is the New Testament, and in particular the four Gospels, which set out to tell the story of his life. But there are also other ancient sources written by those who were either hostile or indifferent to Jesus, which make it clear that he really was a historical figure and not just a figment of the first-century imagination.

Alongside the writings from the time of Jesus there are many new archaeological discoveries. Since the foundation of the state of Israel, the Holy Land has become one large archaeological dig. Scholars cannot resist the opportunity to burrow down below the surface of this most ancient and disputed territory to discover whether there are traces to be found of the events and artefacts described in the Scriptures. Every pilgrim to Israel who visits the holy places is made aware of the hunt for history in the stones and rocks of the land. And every year, it seems, there are new finds, which then have to be analysed, interpreted and added to the growing body of information that is available.

A third source of potential discovery comes from scientists who have an interest in trying to understand some of the events in the Gospels either by coming up with a theory to explain them, or by replicating them under experimental conditions. For historians and Bible scholars, who may have good reasons to doubt whether some of the more extravagantly miraculous events in the Gospels actually happened, this may seem an eccentric approach, but it does yield some interesting and unexpected conclusions. In recent years scientists have given attention to the star of Bethlehem (what was it?), the virgin birth (is there a biological explanation?), the crucifixion (where were the nails driven, and what was the cause of death?) and the resurrection (what drug might have produced an appearance of death?). Not all these experiments and reconstructions are convincing, but they are evidence of our need, as people of the twenty-first century, to make sense of the story that has so shaped Western civilisation.

Putting the landscape of the Holy Land together with both the written evidence about Jesus and the archaeological discoveries about the times in which he lived enables us to construct a much more vivid picture of the gospel story than we have ever had before. For a brief moment, thanks to scholarship, imagination and, often, the ingenuity of computer graphics, we can get a real insight into Jesus' life and times. Though such reconstructions are always open to revision as new facts emerge, they do help us to close the gap of 2,000 years and place ourselves in Jesus' world. And that may be the best way not only of discovering factual information about him, but of deciding whether his message is still relevant to us. And if it is, whether the extraordinary claims made about Jesus in his lifetime and after his death still have the power to change lives.

That's just to set the scene. We now need to look at the sources for Jesus' life in more detail, the main source must be the four Gospels. Taken together they make up almost half of the New Testament. They come one after the other: Matthew, Mark, Luke and John. There's no attempt within the Bible to condense them into one single Gospel, though this is something that was often attempted by later generations of Christians. Nor is there any explanation of why the Gospels differ in detail from one another.

The Gospels are crucial, but just because they come first in terms of order in the New Testament doesn't mean that they are our oldest source. The first person to write about Jesus was his follower and apostle St Paul, who was composing letters to new churches within twenty years of the crucifixion. Maddeningly, Paul gives very little information about Jesus' life and rarely quotes him. Paul speaks of Jesus being born and of the meaning of his death on the cross. His writings are full of a sense of wonder at Jesus' resurrection; it is that belief that drives the apostle. Paul does not tell much of the human story. No doubt he knew the broad outlines of Jesus' life, but it is clear from the New Testament that he never met Jesus in the flesh, and thinks of him primarily as an exalted figure, the Christ sent by God. So

Paul may not be a great help in getting to the historical Jesus. What he does show, though, is how very quickly after his death Jesus came to be worshipped.

The Gospels were written several decades after the events they describe, long after the letters of Paul. This does not mean they are not based on things that really happened. There must have been many eye-witnesses to the main events in the life of Jesus, and there is every reason to assume that genuine memories were preserved and handed on, contributing much to the core of the written Gospels. There were those who heard Jesus preaching, perhaps many times, and became so familiar with his sayings and stories that they could repeat them verbatim.

We can be sure that stories about Jesus changed slightly as they were re-told, to meet the interests of particular listeners. Also in circulation would have been summaries of Jesus' teachings, sayings that he must have repeated many times to different audiences, stories of his own that were remembered, treasured and handed on. Even at such a distance in time it is clear that Jesus was a marvellous story-teller, full of humour, incongruity and vivid detail – always easier to remember than a more bland type of narrative.

Story-telling was a vital element of day-to-day communication in the Middle East of Jesus' time. News came not by newspapers but by messengers, either official heralds or travellers, merchants, traders, soldiers and slaves in the course of their necessary journeys. Telling stories and passing on news would have been an important occupation in that context, and a good memory and a receptive ear were vital social skills. Therefore we can be fairly confident that there is real history in the four Gospels. Some of it will be as it was originally spoken, as fresh on the hundredth telling as it was on the first. Other parts will have been embroidered in various ways.

In fact, we can see pious embroidery at work in small details in the written Gospels. In the story of the empty tomb, for example, Mark describes 'a young man . . . dressed in a white robe' (Mark 16:5) sitting beside the tomb. Matthew has an angel descending from heaven who rolls away the stone to the accompaniment of an earthquake (Matthew 28:2–3), whereas Luke produces 'two men in dazzling clothes' (Luke 24:4). Mark's account is reticent and agnostic. Clearly, the young man is not necessarily an angel. The emptiness of the tomb is not explained. Matthew's account is far more miraculous and pictorial. He tells us explicitly that the angel is a supernatural being. Putting Matthew's and Mark's versions side by side you are left wondering whether Mark's simple account was sensationalised by Matthew, or whether an original sensationalist version was sobered up by Mark to make it all more plausible. Matthew's version would be more compelling, but Mark's would have the possible virtue of reticence, requiring a more profound response of faith. Which is the more authentic? Scholars ask such questions and they are helpful in prodding us to see that the Gospel writers all had slightly different agendas, which made them compose their accounts differently. It used to be believed that the Gospels were written in the order they appear in: Matthew first, then Mark, Luke and John. Today, most scholars think that Mark's Gospel was the first.

Written Gospels were not needed for the first decades of the Christian era, because the followers of Jesus were still in touch with the living memory of those who knew him. You did not need a Gospel when there was old Matthias down the road who knew someone who was *there* when Jesus actually told that story or healed that person. It was only as Christianity began to spread into a world where there was no one still in touch with eye-witnesses that a more permanent record was needed. The Greek word for gospel means 'good news'. It is the kind of news that a herald might bring, news of the arrival of someone important, or of a military victory. The word suggests that the Gospels developed from the preaching of the early Church. It used to be thought that these preached accounts of the life of Jesus were unique, a form of literature that the world had never seen before. In fact, we now know that they take a remarkably similar form to that of other ancient biographies of the Roman world. Lives of emperors, philosophers and military heroes were composed with a sense of high moral purpose, to demonstrate the subject's virtues and to encourage others to emulate them. For this reason, they are highly selective. They rarely include much childhood detail. They concentrate on the big events and draw moral conclusions from them. They include speeches that may never have been made, but express the sentiments the biographer believes would have been appropriate. Such accounts are not interested in the personal psychology of their subjects, in what they felt like or experienced inwardly. What they are concerned with is the *meaning* of the person's life.

The Gospels display many of these traits. They are obviously selective, for they tell us very little about Jesus' childhood, nor, with the possible exception of John, do they attempt to explore his inner experience. They aim not to report objectively, but to teach and proclaim. What is really unique about the Gospels is not their literary genre, but their subject matter. They are biographies of a nobody. Galilean peasants were not a role model for anyone in the first century of the Roman empire. No wonder that in the year AD 363 the Roman emperor, Julian the Apostate, forbade Christians to teach Greek literature. He felt that Christianity had already corrupted classical culture and should not be allowed to ruin it any more: 'If they want to learn literature, they have Mark and Luke: let them go back to their churches and expound them.' Of course, this pagan emperor, who tried to turn the clock back to a time before Christianity was accepted, objected deeply to the Christian message.

There is no evading the fact that the Gospels have a message: they are written to persuade people to have faith in Jesus. They assume, as St Paul did, that Jesus is alive, risen from the dead, and that the resurrection vindicates him as the Son of God, the Messiah of Israel. In that sense, they are a form of religious propaganda. This poses a real problem for many of us today. We are suspicious of rhetoric, of arguments that set out to convince us, of hype. It doesn't help that the Gospels contain accounts of miracles performed by Jesus that many today feel are simply impossible. We do not experience the kind of supernatural events that are reported in the Gospels, and have scientific explanations for many unusual phenomena that were once thought to be the work of God. Because of this, there is a tendency for people to be so sceptical that they discard completely the real historical core of the Gospels.

Yet this is a mistake. There is outside corroboration for the basic outline of Jesus' life, and also for the context in which he lived. Even the fact that we have four Gospels provides us with ways of checking what is most likely to be based on real events and what has been embroidered. From a historian's point of view, more confidence can be put in those incidents, events, stories and sayings that are included in three or more of the Gospels, and perhaps rather less in those recorded only once, or obviously copied from one to another. But the 'once only' rule has exceptions. An incident recorded only in one Gospel and left out of all the others may have been altered or omitted from the others because it was difficult to understand or embarrassing in some way. An example of this is the story of the baptism of Jesus, where Mark clearly has Jesus submitting to John's baptism as a penitent (Mark 1:9–11). For Matthew, this raises embarrassing questions. He doesn't want to think of Jesus as someone with a sense of sin and a need for forgiveness, so he introduces a little dialogue (Matthew 3:13-15) in which Jesus explains that he is only going through the ritual 'to fulfil all righteousness', a vague reason which doesn't imply that Jesus thought he needed baptism to wash away personal guilt.

As far as we know, the Gospel writers worked separately, though there is plenty of evidence to suggest that they shared material. If Mark was the earliest, as most now believe, then Matthew has obviously copied large passages directly from Mark, tidying up some of his work and abbreviating it, but generally only changing a word or two here and there of what Mark provided him with. Matthew also adds a lot of his own material, including the story of Christmas. Luke uses much of the same material as Matthew, but he adapts it more thoroughly, changing the construction and vocabulary to suit his particular purpose and style.

John's Gospel is quite different from the others, though it does contain some of the same incidents. It is more meditative and reflective in style, and it shows a much greater interest in Jesus' own spiritual experience than the other three Gospels. Its outline of Jesus' life is different too. Matthew, Mark and Luke show Jesus spending most of his time in Galilee, and only making one major visit to Jerusalem at the end of his life. John has Jesus making several visits to the Holy City to celebrate Jewish festivals. On the whole, historians find less in John that is historically plausible than in the other three Gospels, though, as always, there are exceptions. For example, John seems to have a more accurate notion of topography and geography than the other writers. In particular, some of his descriptions of Jerusalem fit well both with written evidence from outside the Bible and with what archaeologists have discovered. In chapter 10, John describes Jesus walking in Solomon's portico. The existence of this porch is attested to by other writers. He also sets one of Jesus' miracles beside an ancient pool, which sounds very like the remains of a sacred site near St Anne's Church in the Muslim quarter. There are some who think John's account of the events leading up to Jesus' arrest may be closer to history than the version in the other three Gospels.

However, the evidence of the Gospels for the historical existence of Jesus would not be decisive were it not for other evidence from outside the Christian community. It might be just possible, if unlikely, that someone within the Christian community invented Jesus and that the story circulated and was copied by others with their own variations. But the 'outside evidence' puts paid to this theory.

Jesus was not a well-known or important figure in his lifetime or in the years immediately after his death; however, he is mentioned in passing by two Roman historians. Suetonius, a Roman historian and secretary to the emperor Hadrian until about AD 120, wrote a collection of 'Lives of the Caesars'. In his life of the emperor Claudius he refers to riots among the Jews living in Rome, at the instigation of a certain 'Chrestus'. These riots gave Claudius a good reason to expel the Jews from Rome. Suetonius' account is fairly garbled, but it points to some conflict between Jews and Christians living in Rome about twenty years after the crucifixion. Suetonius is unclear about whether Chrestus was still around or not to inspire the riots, which may point to a genuine confusion, for Christians would no doubt have claimed that the risen Christ, 'Chrestus', *was* still very much around.

Tacitus, another Roman historian who wrote a famous life of his father-in-law Agricola, who once governed Britain, also wrote about Jesus. Writing some eighty years after the death of Jesus, he mentions that he was crucified under Pontius Pilate in the reign of the emperor Tiberius, and refers to his followers as dangerous scum, given to superstition, and hated by all reasonable human beings!

More valuable than these brief references is a portrait of Jesus from a Jewish historian. Josephus was the governor of Galilee thirty years after the crucifixion, when the Jews were rebelling against their Roman rulers. Josephus was captured by the Romans and, realising that the Jewish cause was hopeless, changed sides and became an agent of Rome. He spent the rest of his life in retirement as a Jewish gentleman in Rome, writing the history of the Jews from creation up to his own time. His aim was to defend the Jewish people and their religion. He also wrote an account of the Jewish war against Rome, which he had of course participated in and witnessed closely. Because of Josephus' supposed treachery, until recently scholars have tended to dismiss his testimony as unreliable. Up to a point, they are right to do so, because Josephus had a self-justifying agenda. He set out to show how Jewish defeat was inevitable, but he was also a shrewd and observant reporter and, where he is not busy making his own case, his evidence is extremely useful. He mentions Jesus as a real historical figure:

About this time lived Jesus, a wise man, if he can be called a man. For he worked surprising deeds and was a teacher of such people as accept the truth gladly. He won over many Jews and many of the Greeks. He was the Christ; and when Pilate, on an indictment of the leading men among us, condemned him to the cross, those who loved him from the beginning, did not lose their love. He appeared to them on the third day, alive, in accordance with the holy prophets who foretold not only this, but thousands of other wonderful things about him.

Even to this day the race of Christians, who take their name
from him, has not died out. (Josephus, *Antiquities* xviii, 63)

As it stands, this account cannot be authentic. It makes Josephus
sound like a convinced Christian, which he was not. One
Christian, writing 200 years after Jesus, mentions Josephus as
someone who did not believe in Christ, so he cannot have come
across this passage in this form. What is most likely is that
Christian forgers have doctored the passage. However, many
scholars believe that by removing the obviously christianised
bits, we can get back to what Josephus actually said about Jesus.
He is mentioned only in passing, in the context of a wider
description of conditions in Palestine during the governorship of
Pontius Pilate. The passage, shorn of Christian interpolations,
reads like this: 'About this time lived Jesus, a wise man. He
worked surprising deeds and was a teacher of such people as
accept the truth gladly. He won over many Jews and many of the
Greeks. Upon an indictment brought by leading members of
society Pilate sentenced him to the cross . . .' Scholars believe we
can trust this passage not least because it is so casual. Josephus
had no axe to grind. He mentions Jesus as a minor figure of
interest. It is quite reasonable for Josephus to have called Jesus a
wise man and a teacher of those with respect for the truth.
Elsewhere, Josephus shows a genuine interest in other contemporary figures who were noted for their holiness. The chief
value of Josephus' evidence is that it establishes the main outlines
of Jesus' life independently of the four Gospels. Here, then, is
corroboration of what the Gospels tell us: that Jesus was a miracle
worker and teacher who fell foul of society's leaders and was
ultimately crucified.

Yet beyond this bare outline, how much of the detail given in
the Gospels can we accept as historically true?

1

FROM ANGELS
TO CHROMOSOMES

Bethlehem

Everyone knows that Jesus was born in Bethlehem. Christmas celebrates this fact, with all the familiar accompaniments of shepherds, wise men, a star, angels, oxen, asses and carols. Bethlehem today is an Arab town, a bus ride from Jerusalem, with a thriving street market, several mosques, and a local industry of olive-wood carving for the thousands of tourists and pilgrims who visit the place each year. Bethlehem is famous entirely because of Jesus.

But are the familiar stories about his birth in this 'little town of Bethlehem' really fact or fiction? Doubt may creep in when we realise that, of the four Gospels, only two of them, Matthew and Luke, say that Jesus was born in Bethlehem. John's Gospel reports a conversation among a Jerusalem crowd that suggests many people thought that Jesus was *not* born in Bethlehem

(John 7:40–3). The crowd make the assumption that Jesus could not possibly be the Messiah because he was a Galilean, whereas everyone knew that the Messiah would be descended from David and would come from Bethlehem. (It is quite possible, though, that this conversation is meant ironically. John and his readers were 'in the know' about Jesus' true birthplace.) Going beyond the Gospels, St Paul never mentions Bethlehem and neither do the other New Testament writers. Nor, for that matter, do the Roman historians Suetonius and Tacitus, or even Josephus. So why do Matthew and Luke think that Jesus was born there? Certainly not because Bethlehem was a great or thriving city. In Jesus' time, Bethlehem was a village not far from Jerusalem, probably not much unlike the small Palestinian villages that still exist in the Judean countryside today.

Bethlehem's importance to Matthew and Luke was its historical association with King David, God's chosen monarch who made Israel great. According to the book of Samuel, Bethlehem was a great city of ancient Israel, large enough to have been ruled by its own council of elders. Bethlehem was the home of Jesse of the tribe of Judah, who was David's father. It was where David was born and grew up. David was Jesse's youngest son, and his family duties included looking after the sheep. When the prophet Samuel became disillusioned with Israel's first king, Saul, he was guided by God to Jesse's family in search of a successor. As the youngest, David was nearly overlooked, but when he was eventually summoned, Samuel recognised him as God's chosen, and anointed him with oil as a sign that he would be king.

In time, after Saul's death, David did indeed become king of Israel. He conquered Jerusalem and turned it into his capital. He also bought a site on which to build a shrine for the ancient ark of the covenant, though the temple itself would not be built until the time of his son, Solomon.

David's reign, like that of Saul, was marked by intermittent war with the Philistines. At one point the Philistines held Bethlehem and turned it into a fortified garrison. David, conducting a guerrilla campaign against them in the Judean countryside, once asked his men to bring him a drink from the well of Bethlehem. When they did so, he was overcome by the danger he had put them in, and poured out the water as an offering to God.

Human beings love finding patterns in the past that help to explain or justify the present. It is always fascinating when history appears to repeat itself, especially when the events of an individual's life seem to be mirrored in the life of a descendant. Think of the way political dynasties evolve in particular families: even without a hereditary monarchy, the family of Mahatma Gandhi dominated Indian politics – just as the Kennedy clan continues to obsess Americans. In Britain, people were intrigued to discover that Prince Charles's mistress, Camilla Parker Bowles, was a descendant of a mistress of King Charles II. We are not surprised when history repeats itself; it confirms our sense that there is a pattern, and that providence is working in human events.

What is true for us was also true in the history of the Jews. King David came to be seen as Israel's greatest hero, the ideal monarch. Although the Old Testament histories portray him as far from perfect, and are candid about his moral and political mistakes, he remained in the consciousness of Israel as God's chosen king, a 'son' of God in the sense that God had adopted him and showed him his favour. God also promised that his special love for David would be extended to his descendants. So when in times of trouble the Jews came to long for power and independence, it was natural to hope for a descendant of David to emerge as their leader. This leader would be, like

3

David himself, the 'anointed one', the Messiah.

One of the prophets of the eighth century BC, Micah, even claimed that the Messiah would come from David's city, thus fulfilling God's promises to David all over again in a new era:

> But you, O Bethlehem of Ephrathah, who are one of the little
>   clans of Judah,
> from you shall come forth for me
> one who is to rule in Israel,
> whose origin is from of old,
> from ancient days. (Micah 5:2)

Matthew and Luke were both interested in Jesus' family tree, but they have very different ways of demonstrating his ancestry. Matthew starts with Abraham and goes forward in time, tracing Jesus' ancestors through the patriarchs to David, and then through generations of good and bad kings and important individuals of Davidic descent after the age of the monarchy, until he gets to the father of Joseph, and Joseph himself, Jesus' parent or guardian. Matthew's aim is to show that Jesus is the Messiah, the true descendant of David. Luke, on the other hand, starts with Joseph and works backwards, through David, to Abraham, and then all the way back to Adam, the first man. Luke's aim is to show that Jesus has an even more universal significance. In tracing his line back to Adam, Luke is demonstrating that he is important for the whole human race. Neither of the family trees are real history; they are patterns in the past traced to show who Jesus really is in the design of God. Although Luke and Matthew agree in part on the detail of Jesus' ancestry, there are many names that are quite different. But in spite of their differences, both writers agree that Jesus was indeed the son of David, through Joseph, the husband of Jesus' mother,

Mary. Never mind the fact that they also claim that Joseph was not Jesus' biological father. They were looking for patterns and repeats, and for their purpose Jesus was enough Joseph's son for Joseph's relationship to King David to count. So when they came to name Jesus' birthplace, it would have been natural for them to assume that he was born in Bethlehem. Not only was it fitting for David's descendant to come from his ancestral city; it had been prophesied that he would in fact do so.

Because this explanation is so plausible, many people have assumed that Luke and Matthew were just making it up when they said Bethlehem was the birthplace of Jesus. It is claimed that the two Gospel writers needed this fiction to make sense of their claims about Christ. Because they assumed he was the Messiah, they could read off details of his life from the prophecies made about the Messiah in the Old Testament. He had to be born in Bethlehem because Micah prophesied that he would be. If this argument holds, then the likelihood of Bethlehem being the birthplace of Jesus looks small. Where, then, could he have been born? There is no evidence for anywhere else, but the best bet would be Nazareth, where the Gospels say Jesus grew up.

But Bethlehem should not be dismissed out of hand. It is certainly possible that Joseph came from there, especially if he did have some distant connection with the family of David. Perhaps Mary came from Bethlehem too – after all, they had to meet somewhere! It is also possible that they moved north to Galilee because of social unrest in Judea when Jesus was a small baby. We know there was unrest at this time from the history of Josephus. The story of the massacre of the innocents, though it does not appear in any account other than that of Matthew, does reflect the ruthlessness of King Herod, who at the time of Jesus' birth ruled over the whole of Palestine as a client king of the Romans. So we can well imagine that Joseph and Mary had a home in Bethlehem and then migrated. This reconstruction would fit quite well with Matthew's version of the story, in which Joseph and Mary flee to Egypt with the baby Jesus before settling in Nazareth after Herod's death. Matthew had a particular interest in showing how small details in the story of Jesus appear to fulfil the ancient Hebrew Scriptures. He sees this migration story as a direct fulfilment of some words from the eighth-century BC prophet Hosea, who has God announcing, 'When Israel was a child, I loved him, and out of Egypt I called my son' (Hosea 11:1). Jesus is God's son called out of Egypt, just as ancient Israel was. It is the kind of link-up between old and new that Matthew likes to make.

The assumption that Joseph and Mary migrated from Bethlehem does not fit in nearly so well with Luke's version of Jesus' birth. According to Luke, Mary's home is in Nazareth. It is here that the angel Gabriel comes to announce the birth of Jesus and from here that she went to Bethlehem with Joseph because the emperor had ordered a census requiring everyone to return to their ancestral home. If there had ever been such a census there should have been some record of it in Roman sources, but none appears outside Luke's own account. It sounds suspiciously as though Luke made it up or guessed it as a way of getting Mary and Joseph to Bethlehem. If this is so, then of the two accounts of Jesus' birth at Bethlehem, Matthew's is a little more plausible. At least we can make some connections between it and other contemporary events.

Bethlehem certainly seems to have been accepted without question as the true site of Jesus' birth from early in the Christian era. The Roman emperor Hadrian drove the Jews out of Bethlehem after the second Jewish revolt in AD 135 and built a pagan shrine there, probably in an attempt to prevent the site that was regarded as the birthplace of Jesus from becoming a focus of Christian prayer and pilgrimage. Jerome, the Bible scholar and translator who lived in Bethlehem from AD 386 until his death in 420, wrote that, 'From Hadrian's time until the reign of Constantine [the first Christian emperor] Bethlehem, now ours and the earth's most sacred spot, was overshadowed by a grove of Thammuz, which is Adonis, and in the cave where the infant Messiah once cried, the paramour of Venus was bewailed.' Attempts to repress Christian interest in the site were not wholly successful though. Origen of Alexandria, one of the Church's first real theologians, paid a visit to Bethlehem while he was in Palestine around AD 248 and had the site of the nativity pointed out to him. The way he describes his visit suggests that he was neither alone nor the first to venerate the Saviour's birthplace. It is likely that it was an established site for pilgrimage in spite of being home to a pagan shrine. By AD 326, when Helena, mother of the emperor Constantine, visited the site and built a Christian church on it, no one had any doubt about the exact location of the birthplace of Jesus. It is on the foundation of Helena's original church that the present-day Church of the Nativity now stands. Beneath floor level is the Grotto of the Nativity, a trough that denotes the manger and an ornate star that marks the birthplace.

One thing that is obvious to visitors is that the site is deep in the rock. In fact, Bethlehem and its surrounds are dotted with caves. There is a network of caves under the Church of the Nativity itself. This links in with the intriguing fact that a number of ancient witnesses claim that Jesus was born in a cave, though neither Matthew nor Luke suggest this directly. A clue to understanding this comes from Luke's account, where the child is born in a manger because 'there was no place for them in the inn' (Luke 2:7). We are familiar with the idea of Mary and Joseph turning up exhausted on the doorstep of the inn, only to be banished by the heartless inn-keeper to the

7

stables at the back. But Luke's Greek can mean something quite different. The word translated 'inn' means guest room. It was usually an upper room reserved for visitors. (It is actually the same word that is used for the upper room in Jerusalem where Jesus and his disciples ate the Last Supper.) Beneath the guest room would have been the living quarters and, at the back of the house, the animals would have been sheltered. A cave would have provided ideal shelter, and so we can imagine houses with the living quarters and guest room built in front of and above a cave. If Luke's version does have some historical basis, Mary and Joseph could have been seeking refuge with relations in Bethlehem. Because the guest room was already occupied, they were taken to the cave where the animals lived which would have been quiet and warm.

One can see some of the ingredients of the traditional Christian scene emerging from obscurity. Archaeological investigations have shown that the caves beneath the Church of the Nativity would have been occupied at the time of Jesus. There are traces of hay, seeds and dung, which implies that living, stabling and storage all took place within the same confined space. Of course, this is not to prove the truth of the familiar details of the Christmas story, but it does mean that they cannot be dismissed out of hand.

So though it is probably more likely that Jesus was born in Nazareth, there *is* a case for Bethlehem, which is a little stronger than the evidence of Matthew and Luke alone.

The location of Jesus' birth is only one part of the tradition about him on which new discoveries shed light. But what about two more of the ingredients of Christmas, the wise men and the star?

The wise men

> We three kings of orient are;
> Bearing gifts we traverse afar,
> Field and fountain, moor and mountain,
> Following yonder star.

The wise men are an attractive part of the Christmas tableau. Three travellers, often shown crossing the desert on camels: one from the Far East, one from India, and one from Africa. This story is found only in Matthew's Gospel, and many of the details have been added to by the imagination of poets and artists. Nowhere does Matthew say there were three travellers. It just seems to be a convenient and attractive number, which corresponds to the three gifts Matthew says they brought. They are never described as kings, though there are some verses in the Old Testament that speak of royal kings coming in tribute with gold, which may have influenced the way the story has been told: 'May the kings of Sheba and Seba bring gifts . . . May gold of Sheba be given to him . . .' (Psalm 72:10, 15). 'Nations shall come to your light, and kings to the brightness of your dawn . . .' (Isaiah 60:3).

Some scholars think that Matthew simply made the story up to fit these supposed prophecies, but if he did do this then he might have been expected to use a formula he often employs when he wants to imply that a prophecy is being fulfilled: 'This was to fulfil what the Lord had spoken by the prophet . . .' It is a kind of 'I told you so' remark. But Matthew does not use his favourite formula at this point, either about the wise men or the star they followed. He has the wise men bringing presents of gold, frankincense and myrrh, but he prefers to call the visitors *magi*, which usually means priests who were skilled in

9

astrology. Astrology was widely practised in the ancient world, though it is dismissed in a number of Old Testament writings as a form of idolatry. In the ancient Near East, astrology was associated with Babylonia, the land to the north-east of Palestine, dominated by the twin rivers of the Tigris and the Euphrates. This is present-day Iraq. If Babylonia was the traditional home of astrology, another region where it was also widely known about was ancient Persia, present-day Iran. Both Babylonia and Persia played a political part in the history of the Jews. Babylonia was the place where many leading Jewish families were exiled in the sixth century BC. The Persian kings Cyrus and Darius played an important part in restoring the exiled Jews to their homeland. But even when some exiles had returned, Babylonia remained home for many Jews.

So it is probable that Matthew had in mind astrologer-priests from Persia as his wise men, while being aware that there were prophecies which suggested in general terms that grand visitors might bring gifts to Jerusalem. The magi themselves might have been aware of Jewish predictions of a Messiah-king because of the number of Jews then living in Persia. The case for the Persian origins of the wise men is strengthened by considering the gifts they brought. Gold was a universal precious metal. Myrrh is a bitter, scented oil made from the gum resin of a tree found only in southern Arabia and East Africa. It was used as a cosmetic. It also came to play a part in the ceremonies of anointing kings. It can function as a painkiller and is one of the aromatics used to anoint dead bodies before burial. Frankincense comes from another gum resin, which gives off a strong, sweet, heady smell when burnt. Mixed with herbs to produce incense, it is still used in worship. In ancient times it accompanied sacrifices, its strong scent helping to purify temples and remove the smell of blood.

Frankincense and myrrh, like gold, were precious commodities that were traded between southern Arabia (now the Yemen) and the Levant.

If the wise men really did come from Babylonia or Persia, how did they get hold of their gifts? The only realistic possibility is that they passed a trading centre that would have had supplies of these rare commodities. The most likely stopping place is the ancient caravan city of Petra, now in the south of Jordan. This was the capital and commercial centre of the Nabatean kingdom. At the time of Jesus, the Nabateans were well known as merchant travellers who had settled in Petra. They had an uninterrupted, monarchical form of government, which was virtually independent from Rome. Their prosperity came from the fact that they controlled the major trade route between south and north. They had access to raw materials from far and near, and merchants from India and China sold their produce in their markets. The Nabateans 'added value' by taking raw materials and producing silk, gems, oils, perfumes and pharmaceuticals. By such entrepreneurial efforts they acquired a virtual monopoly on the supply of exotic, luxury goods for the whole region, and their influence was as wide as their commercial success. Frankincense and myrrh were among their most profitable products. Following a caravan route from Persia or Babylonia to Palestine, it is possible that the wise men could have passed close enough to Petra to make a diversion and bought their gifts there. But we have no independent evidence that astrologer-priests from the north did actually pass through Petra at the time of Jesus' birth and make their way to Jerusalem and, from there, to Bethlehem. What discoveries in Petra do show us is that Matthew's story fits plausibly into the political and commercial setting of Jesus' era. If there were real wise men they could well have come from Persia or Babylonia, and if they included frankincense and myrrh among their gifts, they could have done their Christmas shopping in Petra.

The star

The star that the wise men are said to have followed has been the subject of endless speculation. Artists and composers of carols assume it was a particularly bright star, sometimes even shown in the shape of a cross. There are at least two examples in early Christian literature outside the Bible where the star is described as excessively bright. But Matthew never says that the star was particularly bright, rather that it was new. It had not been observed before. So what could it have been? The usual candidates are a fiery-tailed comet, a supernova explosion of a dying star in a distant galaxy, or a rare sighting of some heavenly object, perhaps a planet, which was at that time still unknown.

It was certainly a star with unusual properties. Matthew describes it as going ahead of the wise men until the point where it stood over the place where the child was (Matthew 2:9–10). The only astronomical objects that are ever described in classical literature as moving and then coming to rest are comets, so it is possible that the star of Bethlehem might have been a comet. This was suggested by the early Christian Bible scholar Origen as far back as the third century. There was, in fact, a comet recorded in 5 BC by Chinese astrologers. On the other hand, though comets are occasionally associated with the birth of rulers, they were more often regarded as portents of disaster. The stream of dust and rock that make up the characteristic 'tail' of the comet suggested to some ancient commentators the hair of a hysteric, distracted with grief.

The seventeenth-century astronomer Johannes Kepler believed that the wise men must have seen a supernova, a dying star at the moment when it explodes, spewing molten rock and fiery gas in all directions. There have been some spectacular examples of supernovae appearing in the night sky, including one recorded by Chinese astrologers in the eleventh century that was so bright that it could be seen in daylight. But such remarkable phenomena are not quite in the spirit of Matthew's text. If it had been a supernova, everyone would have noticed and thought that something was up, not least King Herod, whose own wise men were apparently unaware of the new star until the magi told them about it.

It would obviously help if there were any certainty about the birth date of Jesus, but this is not easy to establish. The one thing we can be sure of is that he could not have been born on 25 December of the year AD 1. Our system of dating events from the beginning of the Christian era was only adopted in the sixth century. Before that, Christians kept the same secular dating system as everyone else, with years counted from the foundation of Rome. Unfortunately, the first Christian calendar proved to be four years out, which indicates that Jesus was born in 4 BC. He was certainly born in the reign of the first emperor Augustus, when Herod the Great was ruling Palestine. Herod died in 4 BC, which might suggest that Jesus was born a little earlier, say between 7 and 4 BC. As for the time of year, if there were shepherds present at his birth, it is unlikely that it would have been in the dead of winter. Even in the Holy Land winter nights can be cold and the animals are brought in at that time of year. Spring or autumn are a better bet for when 'there were shepherds living in the fields, keeping watch over their flock by night' (Luke 2:8).

One of the difficulties is that speculation has been based on what a present-day astronomer might find of unusual interest in the night sky. But at the time of the birth of Jesus there was no

13

science of astronomy or astrophysics, no massive telescopes to map the heavens. Astronomy was indistinguishable from astrology, the art of observing and mapping the sky in order to make predictions. Modern scientists tend to dismiss astrology, particularly the predictions on the basis of zodiac signs which make up the 'Your Stars' columns in the newspapers, but in the ancient world it was a kind of science. It was natural to believe that the lives of individuals and nations were connected to the life of the world as a whole, and that human destinies could be read if only you acquired the knowledge to decipher the mysterious script of the night sky.

A number of astronomers interested in the Bethlehem star have begun to look not at astronomical data, but at astrological conjunctions that could have been significant at the time of Jesus. One likely candidate that could fit with Jesus' birth has been suggested by Dr Michael Molnar, an astronomer from New Jersey. He became intrigued by the fact that on 20 March and 6 April in the year 6 BC the moon's orbit of the earth brought it directly in front of the planet Jupiter. This is of no great interest to a modern astronomer, but in the ancient world this would have almost certainly been thought to have had symbolic significance. Jupiter, or Zeus, was the king of the gods, and the planet Jupiter was associated with kingly rule. The event may even have been recorded on an issue of Syrian coinage. Contemporary coins have been found from Antioch in Syria, which show a bust of Jupiter on one side, and a ram gazing at a star on the other. The ram is the sign of Aries, and there is at least one example of Aries being taken as a symbol of Judea. What this adds up to, according to Michael Molnar, is that the conjunction was taken as an unmistakable sign of the birth of a king in Judea. The reason it appears on coinage is perhaps due to the Roman hope that the prophecy would be fulfilled by a Roman. Indeed, it was in a sense, for in AD 6, twelve years after the conjunction, the emperor Augustus assumed control of Judea through a Roman governor – the first to occupy the position that Pontius Pilate would hold. There are two more details that might support this engaging speculation. On the second occasion of the conjunction, 6 April, Jupiter could be seen due east in the night sky, just where Matthew says it was. And it is just possible that Jupiter could have been observed passing through a stationary point, a phase of retrograde motion in its orbit round the sun that would make it appear to hover against the background of stars. An observation of Jupiter doing precisely this was made in 1990. So, perhaps the star did appear to settle for a while over the house where the young child was.

That is Michael Molnar's theory. There is a rival astrological possibility, which is that of a conjunction of Jupiter with Saturn in the constellation of Pisces. Pisces was the sign of the zodiac that represented Israel, and so this would again point to the birth of a king of Israel. This conjunction occurred in May in 7 BC, and if the magi observed it in Persia, it could have been the trigger that propelled them to pack up their camels for the long journey to Palestine. On the way they would have witnessed a spectacular astrological event, when Jupiter and Saturn both rose together at sunset. This theory is given greater plausibility if we translate Matthew's phrase 'We have seen his star in the east . . .' as 'we have seen his star at its rising . . .' (Matthew 2:2). But modern translations often prefer the second version anyway.

Once again, these discoveries do not prove the accuracy of the Christmas story, but they do indicate possible contemporary events that point to its being more plausible than has sometimes been thought. Those for whom the literal truth of the Bible is important might find it disturbing that the literal truth, in this case, might imply a belief in astrology!

The virgin birth

The virgin birth is referred to in two Gospels out of four, so it already has more of a claim to serious attention than the star or the wise men, which appear only in one. Not only is it part of the gospel story, it is an article of the Church's faith, mentioned in the Creed. Yet for many people this is a serious sticking point. In human beings, virgin births just don't happen. Or do they? This is an area, surely, where modern biology and genetics could shed some light. After the cloning of Dolly the sheep in 1997, we are perhaps wrong to dismiss unusual examples of reproduction.

One scholarly objection to bringing science into the discussion is that the virgin birth is better explained as a misunderstanding. It appears to be an example of an Old Testament prophecy fulfilled. Matthew quotes Isaiah 7:14 as an 'I told you so' fulfilment of a prophecy: 'Behold, a virgin shall conceive and bear a son, and his name shall be called Emmanuel' (Matthew 1:23, Revised Standard Version). Surely Matthew has just lifted the text and then provided an enchanting story that shows that the prophecy has been fulfilled? And in lifting the text he has got it wrong. The word he translates as virgin simply means 'young woman', and it doesn't convey the miraculous meaning that he wants it to. (The word is translated 'young woman' in the New Revised Standard Version.) This argument has some weight, but the suggestion that the Hebrew word for virgin can be translated in this context to mean what the objectors want it to mean – that is, simply a young woman, presumably respectably married – is also open to question. In the Middle East there is a clear distinction between a virgin, and a wife or mother. It is assumed that unmarried women must be virgins. The word used by Isaiah and quoted by Luke more naturally means a woman before she is married. Also, the Greek version of the text uses a word that translates best as virgin.

Yet even if the objections to Matthew's story are sound, we also have to reckon with the fact that Luke has his own virgin birth story, including the visit of Gabriel and the birth in the manger, and he doesn't quote the Isaiah text at all. The tradition that there was something strange about the birth of Jesus carries weight because it has come in two distinct versions that do not appear to have influenced each other at all. In fact, they contradict at various key points, such as where Mary and Joseph came from.

Therefore simply writing off the story as a biblical howler, as some (including a few bishops) have been inclined to in recent years, will not do. It might confirm our sense of family propriety for Jesus to be the natural child of Joseph and Mary, but the evidence that he was is not very strong.

So what was it that was irregular about the birth of Jesus? Perhaps he was illegitimate, or there was some other complication in determining his paternity. Illegitimacy could well have been regarded as a serious handicap. First-century society was firmly patriarchal. Women had far less status and power than men. Pregnancy outside marriage would have had dire consequences for the mother. Nadera Shalhoub-Kervorkian, who works for the Israeli Institute of Criminology and Social Work, believes that we can deduce what attitudes to illegitimacy must have been in the time of Jesus from today's Palestinian society. A young woman who becomes pregnant outside marriage today is still likely to be shunned from society. The father of her child has not only ruined her, but has severely insulted and damaged the honour of her family. The young woman herself is in danger. She may be murdered or imprisoned or driven to commit suicide to redress the honour of the family. If her pregnancy is the result of rape, the aggressor may be forced to marry her. If she is in a romantic relationship there may be violent reprisals against her lover. These attitudes are not confined to the Middle East or to peasant societies. It is not so long ago that even in Britain girls who became pregnant outside marriage were regarded as morally degenerate and could find themselves confined to mental institutions. There are parallels to these harsh attitudes in the Gospels. Matthew suggests that when Joseph discovered that Mary was pregnant his immediate reaction was to call off the marriage. But being an (unusually) just man (as Matthew puts it), Joseph did not want to disgrace her; instead, he planned to cancel the marriage arrangement quietly. When Joseph reluctantly accepted Mary's account of how she had become pregnant, he went ahead and married her and took steps to conceal the circumstances of the birth (Matthew 1:19–25).

The awkwardness about the birth of Jesus can also be deduced from looking at other evidence from the Gospels. Matthew's genealogy traces Jesus' ancestors back to King David, and before him to the patriarch Abraham. Matthew describes Joseph rather unconvincingly as 'the husband of Mary of whom Jesus was born'; Luke goes one step further and says that Joseph was the father 'as was supposed' of Jesus. In spite of building up an impressive list of ancestors, both writers end their genealogies with a heavy suggestion that Jesus was not, in fact, genetically related to the forebears who have just been listed. In the ancient world this would not have been quite so odd as it seems to us, as adoption was widely practised and did confer some sense of real participation in the family into which one had been adopted. But you cannot help getting the impression that the genealogies conceal as much as they reveal.

Matthew is particularly interested in a group of female ancestors, all of whom produced heirs as a result of irregular relationships. He mentions Tamar, Ruth and the wife of Uriah the Hittite. Tamar became pregnant by her father-in-law who thought she was a prostitute and picked her up for casual sex. She had originally been promised to one of his sons in marriage and, to her disappointment, the marriage never took place. Her pregnancy exposed the duplicity with which she had been treated and she made sure that her father-in-law knew about it! She gave birth to twins. Ruth was a non-Israelite, a Moabite woman, who followed her Israelite mother-in-law, Naomi, back to her homeland, and made a good marriage to a relative of her mother-in-law after seducing him at a harvest supper. The wife of Uriah the Hittite was the beautiful Bathsheba. King David fell in love with her, and when he spied on her bathing, he arranged for her husband to be killed so that he could marry her.

Why does Matthew highlight the fact that these women are forebears of Christ? The reason could be that the stories of these three women all tell of sexual relationships that are in some way irregular, but that not only turned out well in the end, but also forwarded God's purpose. So, Matthew implies, Jesus' birth was in continuity with a divine plan that had already bent the normal rules of marriage and legitimacy. In the light of these past patterns it makes sense for the Messiah to be born in an unusual way. A virgin birth is not to be interpreted as a scandal, but as the miraculous fulfilment of an ancient promise.

What is also interesting is that though the Gospels refer to Jesus as the son of Joseph (Luke 4:22; John 6:42), there is evidence that he was also known as the son of Mary (Mark 6:3). This is much more unusual. In peasant communities it is obvious and normal to call people by the father's name, as a kind of surname. We know in English how many surnames end in 'son' – Johnson, Davidson, Richardson, etc. But for Jesus to be called 'son of Mary' suggests that his contemporaries knew that his relationship with Joseph was not straightforward. Mark's Gospel describes people who are astonished at the eloquence with which Jesus has been teaching in the synagogue, exclaiming, 'Is not this the carpenter, the son of Mary, and brother of James and Joses and Judas and Simon, and are not his sisters here with us?' Matthew repeats Mark's story, with a little of his characteristic tidying up, in Matthew 13:55.

Another piece of evidence that speaks against Joseph being Jesus' natural father is a sneering reference in John's Gospel when a Jewish crowd insist that 'we are not illegitimate children', as though to suggest that Jesus is (John 8:41). This may well reflect suspicions that emerged about Jesus' legitimacy as Christianity began to make an impact. One Jewish story claimed that he was fathered by a Roman soldier.

All this suggests that the story of Jesus' unusual origins may have more historical substance behind it than has often been thought. And, in the light of that, it is worth looking to contemporary science to see if there are any possible explanations of this miracle of miracles. We need to remember that Matthew and Luke probably had different assumptions about human reproduction from our scientific ones. In the ancient world it was commonly believed that when a woman conceived, the male sperm acted as the *agent* of pregnancy, but that the *material* that developed into a new life was solely contributed by the woman. What the male provided was the basic force that transformed material from the mother's body into a new life. So when Matthew and Luke speak of Mary conceiving by the Holy Spirit, they are not implying that the Holy Spirit provided new genetic material or that God was literally Jesus' biological father. They were not aware that two sets of material were needed to make a new human person.

The individual who has done most work to make sense of the virgin birth in terms compatible with science is Sam Berry, a professor of genetics at University College, London. Sam Berry is a convinced Christian who has an idiosyncratic view of miracles. He doesn't think they are beyond explanation, more that they are simply extremely unusual. They show God acting through nature in exceptional ways. Therefore he has looked for examples in nature that might explain the virgin birth. One obvious example is the phenomenon of parthenogenesis, which means, literally, 'virgin birth'. This occurs naturally in about one in a thousand species. Bees, frogs and worms are known to reproduce in this way. It means that eggs begin dividing and developing of their own accord, without fertilisation, and eventually produce a new individual. There is evidence that unfertilised human eggs do occasionally begin dividing and will produce primitive bone and nerve tissue, but the process rarely gets far. Muscle tissue is not produced, and the result is a bizarre tumour, a tetroma, which may show signs of hair and even teeth, but is incapable of becoming a human being.

Parthenogenesis is unknown in humans (though there have been wacky claims from time to time). But could the birth of Jesus be the one exception, the supreme example of God acting in an unusual way? Unfortunately, no. If he had been conceived by parthenogenesis, Jesus would have been a girl. This is because the gender of individuals is determined by the chromosomes they inherit from their parents. Women pass on X chromosomes, and men pass on either X or Y. In normal reproductive intercourse girls are conceived when the male sperm adds a second X chromosome to the ovum; boys when the sperm adds a Y chromosome. So somehow it has to be explained how Jesus received a Y chromosome.

One possibility is that Mary was unusually constituted so as to possess both an X and a Y chromosome. We know that this does

21

occasionally happen, through a freak mutation. If this was the case with Mary, then she could have appeared to be female, and yet have carried the male sex gene. The problem is that such women are usually sterile and don't even have a womb. So they would be unable to give birth at all. But, Sam Berry argues, these freak women are all unique and show enormous variation in the size and characteristics of their sexual organs. He believes that it is not impossible, given these variations, that a woman carrying a Y chromosome could have developed a normal womb and given birth to a son.

Another variation on this possibility that Sam Berry has developed is that Jesus was a male with two X chromosomes. Again, this is not unknown in nature. It can happen when the bit of the Y chromosome that determines male development gets attached to another chromosome in the mother. If the important gene from the Y chromosome had become attached to one X chromosome, and this had not been activated in childhood, Mary would have been female but would have been able to pass on the male determining gene along with two X chromosomes. He points out that men with two X chromosomes are sterile, but in Jesus' case, he suggests, this would not matter. We can never know whether or not he was fertile as he apparently never married or attempted to produce children. Even with two X chromosomes he would still be a real man; he would even be 'perfect man' in the theological sense that Christian doctrine implies when it speaks of Jesus as truly human and truly divine at one and the same time.

As Sam Berry himself says, the point of all this speculation is not to provide a mechanism for understanding the virgin birth so much as to show that it is not completely outside the scope of biological imagination; it just could have happened. But his suggestions raise a further problem. They put Jesus into the realm of the biologically freaky. Whether he can be seen as 'perfect man' if he was produced by such exotic means is open to question.

The virgin birth became an important part of Christian faith because it was taken as proof that Jesus really was human, not a god in disguise or a manifestation of some cosmic power. As the first Christians saw it, he was not only the Son of God, but he was also truly one of us, born of a human mother in exactly the same way as all human babies are. Whether a supposed freak birth really conveys what the Christmas story intends is not obvious.

So, the truth about the virgin birth remains elusive. Science shows that it is just within the realm of possibility, and the Gospels seem to hint that there was some irregularity about the birth of Jesus. On the basis of this, some argue that the hostility evoked by suspicions that Jesus was not Joseph's son would have been played down by the early Christians. They would have wanted Jesus to appear respectable and would have done their best to 'lose' the story. The fact that Matthew and Luke stuck to it argues for its truth. This is interesting, but perhaps a bit naïve, because by the time Matthew and Luke were writing, the Christian gospel had reached beyond Palestine into non-Jewish Greek-speaking communities where a virgin birth would have been considered not so much scandalous as fascinating.

We know from Paul's letters how quickly after the crucifixion Christianity started to attract converts from among the pagans as well as Jews in the towns and cities and commercial centres of the Roman empire. Even the Jews who came from these backgrounds would have had some familiarity with Greek and Roman myths of gods impregnating virgins and giving birth to heroes. It is possible that the story passed on by Luke and Matthew would have found a sympathetic hearing among those who knew the Greek myths. Not because it copies them, but because it is so different. Where the myths tell of gods raping attractive maidens and producing warriors, the Gospels describe the conception of Jesus by the action of the Holy Spirit and the willing acceptance of an unimportant peasant girl. The story would have moved people because it speaks of a God who comes down from heaven in humility, not a lust-driven Olympian who zaps people without becoming vulnerable himself. The reason the virgin birth story goes on resonating is that it is consistent with the rest of Jesus' life and teaching. It is about God being interested in the poor and the unimportant. It has inspired the disadvantaged to realise that they have human dignity, and it has (sometimes) challenged rich and powerful people to live lives of humility and service. The story has spiritual mileage, even if it is dodgy historically. If the way we explain it fails to express that, then perhaps we've missed the point and should regard it, as most do, as a matter of faith. Either you get it, or you don't – like so much about Jesus and his story.

2

From Nazareth
to the Desert

Jesus was a real historical figure, whose life and death follows the broad outline of the gospel story, an outline that is confirmed by the Roman historians Suetonius, Tacitus and, most importantly, the Jewish writer who was his near contemporary: Josephus.

Jesus and his home town

Jesus was brought up in Nazareth. This was such a well-known fact to his contemporaries that he became known simply as Jesus of Nazareth. This was the name under which he was crucified (John 19:19). He was also known to some as 'the Nazarene', a name that was later transferred to his followers. Nazareth is not mentioned in the Old Testament and was not a place of any previous significance. We don't know whether Mary and Joseph originally came from there, as Luke's Gospel implies, or whether they moved there when Jesus was a baby, as could be deduced from Matthew's Gospel. They certainly had relatives there. Matthew records a conversation in which 'sisters' are mentioned in Nazareth who are not part of the immediate family (Matthew 13:6). It is possible that Luke knew about an extended family network in Nazareth, so he assumed that Mary and Joseph must have come from there originally, but it is equally possible that Mary and Joseph were Bethlehem people who moved to Nazareth.

Matthew tells us that they fled from Bethlehem soon after the birth of Jesus to avoid King Herod's hunt for the king of the Jews. Egypt, to the south, would have been an obvious place of refuge until the troubles were over. After Herod's death they may have felt they stood a better chance of stability in Galilee. They may also have been drawn by the prospect of work. Not far from Nazareth, a major city was being built called Sepphoris. Perhaps Joseph saw the opportunities for a carpenter to make a decent living for a few years while the city was being constructed. Either way, no one seriously doubts that Nazareth was the setting of Jesus' boyhood. It was his home town, where he grew up, where he learnt his ancestral faith, where he probably worked as an apprentice to Joseph in the carpentry trade.

But perhaps the most important thing about Nazareth is that it was in Galilee.

Galilee

Growing up in Galilee will have shaped Jesus in important ways. Galilee was not the heartland of Jewish life; it was in the north, several days' journey from Judea. Compared with Judea, Galilee was marginal, too far from the temple and from the seat of power to be important. Life moved at a slower pace. There had been Gentiles living in Galilee long before the time of Jesus, and for this reason it was known as 'Galilee of the nations' (Isaiah 9:1). But although there were Greek cities in Galilee from the third century BC, it was far from being a wholly Gentile region, unlike the areas to the north and east across the Jordan that were heavily populated by non-Jews. The Jews of Galilee may have been descended from the northern Israelites and preserved their special traditions. Because of its distance the temple was less important to most Jews of Galilee than it was to the Jews of Judea. Galilean Jews were in some ways more like Jews in other parts of the Roman empire, like Antioch.

Jesus grew up as a Jew, but in a pluralistic world. He would have known Jews and non-Jews. Of the non-Jews, some would have been natives; others would have moved there seeking work or to pursue commercial interests. Archaeologists have discovered evidence of imported pottery from all round the Mediterranean and the Aegean. So we are probably right to think of Galilee as both more open to the outside world than Judea, and at the same time more rural, conservative and less likely to be inflamed by fervent nationalism. The effect of this pluralistic background would probably have produced mixed feelings in Jesus about non-Jews. On the one hand, he would have been familiar with them; on the other, he may have been wary of compromising the traditions of his own people. Some of this ambivalence is reflected in the Gospels.

Nazareth today

Nowadays people visit Galilee to explore the landscape of Jesus' childhood and early adulthood. Today it is a fairly short run from Jerusalem, partly by motorway and then by main road. Nazareth is roughly equidistant from the Mediterranean coast and the Sea of Galilee. It is a major city with a number of important local industries including electronics. It doesn't look like an important historical centre and, disappointingly for tourists and pilgrims, there are few ancient remains on view. It is also a tense city. Jews, Arabs and Christians all have competing interests here. In recent years there has been a smouldering dispute about a new mosque which is being built right next to the modern Catholic Basilica of the Annunciation.

The one thing that has not changed, though, is the landscape. Nazareth is built on a hill, so it is quite hard work on the feet for today's visitors, who come here in droves. The hill is mentioned in Luke's Gospel (Luke 4:29). At the beginning of his ministry Luke tells us that Jesus preached in the synagogue at Nazareth, boldly taking a text from Isaiah which foretold the coming of the Messiah. As Luke tells us, this was a deeply provocative thing to do and the congregation was angry to the point of seizing Jesus and hauling him up to the top of the hill with the intention of throwing him off the edge. He managed to escape, though Luke does not say exactly how! But regardless of whether the incident occurred as Luke describes it, the story does suggest that the village was near the summit of the hill that the modern city is now built on.

In spite of the lack of obvious remains, the cluster of churches in Nazareth do reveal clues about what the place was like at the time of Jesus. Under the foundation of a church dedicated to St Joseph, which was built in 1914 over the remains of a medieval church, an underground cave has been found. This encloses passageways to storage chambers at an even lower level. These were probably used for storing grain, and provide evidence that this village was occupied by a farming community. Unfortunately it is impossible for further excavations to be carried out because the site is built over, but archaeologists think that at the time of Jesus there could have been up to 1,500 people living there – a small enough community for all faces, at least, to be familiar. No wonder when Jesus stood up in the synagogue and announced the fulfilment of Isaiah's prophecy he got a drubbing at the hands of his elders and betters.

Ever keen to interest the streams of modern tourists, archaeologists and local businesses are currently sponsoring an attempt to re-create peasant houses as they might have been at the time of Jesus. It also helps visitors to feel they have seen something authentic-looking, as there isn't much else for the imagination to take hold of.

As a carpenter, Joseph would have been much in demand in Nazareth, whether or not he also took on work in Sepphoris. In a farming community tools have to be kept in order, there are carts and barns to be built, and repairs carried out on roofs and doorways. Joseph would have known everyone, and Jesus would have grown up in a busy household. There is an obvious devotional tendency to think of the home of Jesus as a haven of calm and quiet happiness, and that the holy family were poor but content. But it is more probable that Jesus grew up in an atmosphere of insecurity. There are certainly some historians who believe that Joseph may have taken to carpentry because he lost his own land as part of a movement in which richer landlords bought up the plots worked by independent peasant farmers. We know that this happened both in Judea and in Galilee at the time of Jesus, so there may have been domestic worries about work, debt and survival.

Jesus was not an only child. The Gospels mention brothers and sisters. These may have been legitimate children of Mary and Joseph or, as pious tradition has always insisted, children of a former marriage of Joseph's, or even cousins. (The pious tradition protects the belief that Mary remained a virgin after her marriage to Joseph.)

Jesus' missing childhood

We are naturally curious about the childhood of Jesus because we accept the findings of psychology: that childhood plays a large part in forming our character and temperament. We want to know what were the most formative influences on Jesus' life. Did he know about the circumstances of his birth? Did Mary tell him about an angel and a promise that he would be a man of destiny, or did she keep it to herself? Did she teach him to pray or help him to read? Could she read herself? One thing we do know, though, is that the family would have spoken Aramaic, the language of Syria that was also spoken in Palestine. If Jesus accompanied his father to Sepphoris, he may also have needed to manage in Greek, which was the everyday language of public life and commerce. If he learnt to read, he would have needed to master Hebrew, at least well enough to read in the synagogue assembly. Another thing we can safely assume is that Jesus would have been circumcised as a baby. Luke tells us this specifically (Luke 2:21), but even if he hadn't we could have taken it for granted, since it was the most important mark of Jewish identity.

And what about playtime? Childhood in peasant societies is not a time of enchantment and discovery. Jesus would have spent his babyhood with his parents working all hours, perhaps farmed out to older relatives, though not many would have lived beyond fifty. When he was big enough he would have been expected to help, no doubt with his father's trade, but also in the fields with the farmers and looking after the sheep. No doubt there were also times for play, and Jesus and his brothers and sisters would have messed about with leather balls and had their own make-believe games as children always do.

The silence of the Gospels about the childhood of Jesus

simply reflects the fact that the writers did not feel it was very important. Their purpose was to proclaim him as Son of God and Saviour, and this purpose shaped the way they edited the memories handed down to them. Like today's journalists, they wanted the Gospels to be relevant to their readers and to resonate with their concerns. Childhood was not sentimentalised in the ancient world. When you think of the numbers of babies who died in infancy and children who never reached adulthood, it does not seem unreasonable to assume that childhood was something to be survived before real life could begin.

But once a community had formed that worshipped Jesus as the Son of God, curiosity developed about the life of this divine child before the events recorded in the biblical Gospels. There is plenty of later Christian literature, in the form of additional gospels not in the Bible, which purports to tell of incidents in Jesus' childhood. These gospels present him as a solemn, precocious child, smugly aware of his divine status and performing miracles to fearful and admiring audiences of his contemporaries. Such accounts are the product of a fervent religious imagination, but they have no historical value.

However, the stories about Jesus' infancy and boyhood, sparse though they are, may have contributed something in the long term to the way in which Christian culture came to value childhood. It is still an astonishing and moving claim that the Son of God could be born in a humble stable and cry and feed like any other baby. Not only does it make God seem more approachable, but it gives a dignity to the beginning of human life that has not been present in all cultures. In the ancient world, Christians and Jews stood out against the common practices of abortion and infanticide.

Luke fills in the gaps

The one Gospel that contains a more extensive treatment of Jesus' childhood is the Gospel of Luke. Luke not only spells out that the infant Jesus was circumcised when he was eight days old, he also tells of a visit Mary, Joseph and Jesus made to the temple in Jerusalem for a purification ceremony while he was still a baby (Luke 2:22–40). This is a beautiful account of the meeting with the old man Simeon, who prophesies that Jesus will be the salvation of Israel. But there are reasons to doubt its authenticity. Although Luke is very keen to show his knowledge of Jewish law and customs (he was a Gentile himself), he makes a mistake. The Jewish understanding of purification after childbirth involves only the mother, not the (supposed) father, nor the infant. The mother, if she went to Jerusalem, would have gone to a special court in the temple reserved for women alone and offered a sacrifice at the end of the period after the birth during which she would have been confined to the home. The ritual marked her return to full participation in society after the ritual uncleanness that accompanied childbirth. The turtledoves, or pigeons, that Luke mentions were the offerings of poor people. Those who could afford it would have offered a lamb.

The story is important to Luke's purpose, which is to show that Jesus was brought up by observant, faithful Jews. Luke has his own agenda, though, which is to show that there was no incompatibility between the new faith and the Roman empire. He sees a continuity between Jewish faithfulness and the development of Christianity, and so he wants to show the temple as a benign part of Jewish and Christian life. So he places Jesus in the temple right from the beginning. Luke was a superb story-teller. He knew that the confrontation with those who ran the Jewish temple was the crisis that led to Jesus' arrest and death, so he wants to make it quite clear that from his point of view Jesus comes from a family that revered and honoured the temple and its traditions. Luke is such an attractive narrator, and his scene setting and character drawing are so convincing, that it comes as a bit of a let-down to realise that some of his best moments are more art than history.

The visit to the temple

This point needs to be remembered in the context of another story of Jesus' boyhood. Luke tells us that Mary and Joseph made an annual visit to Jerusalem in the company of friends and relatives at Passover time, and when Jesus was twelve he was taken with them. If the story does reflect an actual historical incident, it will have been the first time that Jesus actually saw the temple. It would have been a new and exhilarating experience for a poor boy from a country village. The journey from Galilee would have taken several days, and would have ended in a long climb up from the Jordan valley to the sloping hills that surround Jerusalem. On the way the pilgrims would have sung psalms, praising the beauty of God's holy city. And it *was* a beautiful city; King Herod's extravagant building programme had transformed it into one of the most impressive Roman-style cities in the eastern part of the empire. What would the boy Jesus have made of the temple itself?

It would have been an overwhelming sight. The Jewish temple was famed throughout the ancient world, and part of this fame was due to its uniqueness. There was only ever one Jewish temple, though most of the cults followed in the Roman empire had a temple in every city. The Jewish temple was similar in design to other temples, consisting of a series of courts that led to a place of sacrifice and an inner sanctuary. In pagan temples this sanctuary housed the image of the divinity in whose honour the temple was built. In Solomon's temple the ark of the covenant had been in the innermost shrine, a chest shaped like a throne containing the Ten Commandments. It indicated the invisible presence of God. After the exile, the Jewish temple had nothing in its innermost sanctuary, the 'holy of holies', but it was still believed to be the place where God was present.

So the temple Jesus would have visited was the second to be constructed on the same site. Solomon's original one had been built on a natural mound that had originally been a threshing floor. The story of the choice of the site is curious. King David had attempted to hold a census of his subjects; this had angered God, who sent a plague on the people. David then repented, and the angel of the plague halted its progress beside Araunah the Jebusite's threshing floor. David then bought the threshing floor from Araunah, and built an altar there. Solomon's temple housed Israel's greatest treasure, the ark of the covenant. The temple lasted from the middle of the tenth century BC until 586 BC when it was destroyed by the Babylonians. The ark was lost at this time and never recovered. Many leading families of Judah were taken into captivity in Babylonia, and it was not until the exiles began to return, under the protection of the King of Persia, that the temple was rebuilt. Today there are no traces of Solomon's original structure. If they exist, they are buried under the huge platform that Herod built to accommodate his massively extended sanctuary.

Josephus tells us that Herod had lavished money on the temple. But now, through the discoveries of archaeologists, we are beginning to see how Josephus' written record is matched by discoveries in stone. Herod had built a huge stage to extend the area on which the temple perched. He managed to construct a flat surface by building high walls on each side to the height of the crest of the mount. He then filled in the gaps to create a smooth surface. The temple was now positioned to soar over the two valleys on either side, buttressed by the new walls which rose up from the valley floor. Herod's foundations were so strong that they still exist; the mighty platform can be admired in all its dimensions to this day. The platform was framed by covered porticoes, the one to the south side being wider than the others. This was the royal portico, and was the entrance for the priests, traders and bureaucrats who worked within the temple precincts.

Herod's building programme required thousands of labourers and had solved the city's unemployment problem at a stroke. Once the main structures were in place there was scope for skilled craftsmen and artisans to design and execute the delicate porticoes, gates and arches that surrounded the central sanctuary. The royal portico, which ran across the south end of the complex, was divided into three sections by four rows of carved pillars. The tops of the pillars tapered into carved foliage and the ceiling was decorated with leaves and flowers.

This was the site of the temple bank, the porch of the money-changers, and of traders who sold animals and birds for sacrifice. The business side of the life of the temple was concealed from the average pilgrim who entered the temple by a staircase that ran underneath the royal portico. Nevertheless, it was the centre of the temple's economic life, the source of its vast treasuries, and of the wealth of those priestly families who ran the shrine.

The sanctuary itself was gilded. This was the sacred heart of Judaism, the series of courts that no non-Jew could enter on pain of death. A magnificent gate led into the court of the women; beyond that, no woman could go. Further in was the place where sacrificial animals were slaughtered, surrounded by drains to sluice away the blood. There was the altar for burnt offerings, the altar of incense, the golden table for the bread of the presence, and the seven-branched lampstand, the menorah. The holy of holies was entered only once a year, by the High Priest on the day of atonement. This was the place of forgiveness, where the High Priest could come with the sacrificial blood and plead forgiveness for the sins of the year. It guaranteed the special relationship God had with his people.

Jesus meets the teachers

Luke says nothing about what impact all this had on Jesus, but he does tell a curious story about the end of the visit. Mary and Joseph had set off with their relations to return to Galilee, when they found that Jesus was not among their party. Returning in panic to the city, they eventually found Jesus in earnest conversation with the teachers and doctors of the law, listening to them and asking them questions. It is Luke's way of showing that Jesus was highly intelligent, orthodox and competent as a scholar and teacher from adolescence onwards. But this doesn't quite ring true. The Jerusalem temple would not have been a setting in which a country boy with a thick accent could have had a sophisticated conversation with some of the top theological brains of his time; they would not have given him the time of day. However, Luke is right in one respect. There are Jewish writings from the first century that suggest that the steps that led up to the temple were a place for theological argument and debate. These steps have been found and renovated; and it is quite possible that if Jesus did make a visit there with his family, he overheard some of the talk of the scholars and was inspired by it. Jesus might have begun to sense the deep rift at the heart of the Jewish world, between those who were passionately seeking the reign of God, and those for whom Jewish identity was inextricably linked to the temple cult.

That is all we know about Jesus' childhood and it does not add up to much. For about the next eighteen years of his life, all our sources are silent. Luke tells us that he was obedient to Joseph and Mary after his disobedience in Jerusalem, and we can only assume that he continued to live with Mary and Joseph and their extended family in Nazareth. Joseph probably died at some point, though no one mentions it. There is no evidence that Jesus married, though it cannot be ruled out completely. The only thing we can assume is that Jesus was not unaware of the political and religious tensions of his time and place. We know about these only indirectly from the Gospels, but we can deduce much more from Josephus' writings and recent archaeology.

Sepphoris

Not many Bible commentaries mention the city of Sepphoris. It is never spoken of in the Gospels, and if we only had them for evidence we would never have connected it with Jesus. But it was only four miles away from Nazareth, just over an hour's walk; Sepphoris was a big Roman town that, for much of Jesus' childhood, would have resembled a building site. When Jesus was a baby, Sepphoris had been a focus for violent unrest. This had accompanied the death of Herod the Great in 4 BC, when Jesus was (if he was born in about 6 BC) just two years old. Herod had been a great monarch in many ways, but at the same time he was a ruthless manipulator who made many enemies. There was no one in his immediate family who could replace him; his will divided Palestine between his sons. But the succession was never going to be a smooth one. The sons plotted against one another, and there was civil war. Josephus tells us that in Galilee there was a revolt led by a pretender to Herod's throne, Judas son of Hezekiah, who broke into the royal armoury and armed his followers. His revolt was put down with the help of Roman soldiers marched in from Syria. Sepphoris was burnt to the ground.

The Romans re-established order elsewhere as well. Herod's son Archelaus had failed to keep the peace in Judea, and after two years he was deposed and replaced by a Roman governor. Another more capable son of Herod then took over as Tetrarch of Galilee. One of his first projects was to rebuild the ruined city of Sepphoris. He set up his residence in the city and embarked on a twenty-year renovation programme, determined to create a thriving commercial city in the Roman style. He didn't remain in Sepphoris permanently, but moved his capital to Tiberias on the coast, where another Roman urban centre was created.

But in the years of Jesus' late childhood and early manhood, Sepphoris would have been a bustling, thriving, expanding centre. It was designed on the Roman pattern, which was a grid system with a main street running through the centre and subsidiary routes at right angles. There was a forum and public baths. The layout and design of buildings would have been familiar to any soldier, merchant or traveller in the Roman world. It is impossible to believe that Jesus didn't visit the city – perhaps to get supplies, perhaps to seek work. It would have been his first encounter with the culture of Rome. He would have become familiar with the idea of people stripping off and bathing in the nude, both of which would have been an affront to Jewish sensibilities. He would have seen luxury items for sale that were beyond the wildest dreams of the hard-pressed peasants. But though Sepphoris was to all appearances a Roman city, it still seems to have had a predominantly Jewish population. Archaeologists deduce this from the fact that when they have cut down to the layers that represent the first century, they have been unable to find any pig bones. Pork, apparently, was banned in accordance with Jewish food laws. Later layers of remains do reveal pig bones, reflecting the cosmopolitan population of a later era. But at the time of Jesus this essential prohibition was widely, perhaps universally, accepted in Sepphoris. There is every reason to assume that Sepphoris would have introduced Jesus to a kind of Jewishness that was comfortable with Roman culture and Roman ways while at the same time maintaining strict religious separation. The fact that Jesus is never reported as having visited Sepphoris during the years of his ministry suggests strongly that he did not like what he found there.

The excavation of Sepphoris has taken place over the last twenty years. A number of fascinating discoveries have indicated the presence of rich, priestly families in the town, who would have had strong links with the temple in Jerusalem. One suggestive find is a number of ceramic incense shovels, which look like copies of the bronze originals used in the temple. A large number of stone vessels have also been found of a style associated with ritual hand-washing. Similar vessels are described in the second chapter of St John's Gospel in the story of the wedding at Cana in Galilee. Stone was thought of as inherently pure, unlike pottery, metal or glass – which all needed ritual immersion to be pure.

But perhaps most significant is the large number of ritual baths that have been found, including one spectacular example discovered inside the remains of a first-century house. The bath is in a vaulted room, a kind of rock-clad bathroom. It is designed for running water and drainage. It uses rainwater from the roof. It is a perfect example of the kind of bath a priestly family would have needed to maintain ritual purity. It would have washed away defilement from crockery and cutlery so that they were ritually pure for the Sabbath. It provided a place of purification for the priest if he came into contact with a corpse or a dead animal. It would have been where a priest's wife and daughters would have immersed themselves after menstruation. According to Eric Meyers, a veteran of archaeological sites in Galilee, this strongly suggests that 'the people living here were very much focussed upon ritual impurity and how to rid themselves of it'. Purity laws were very much part of the law-code of ancient Israel. They existed to define what is holy and to separate it from what was polluted or profane. Jesus would have taken much of this for granted. He would not have eaten pork or shellfish. He would have washed frequently, not so much for reasons of hygiene, as to maintain the holiness before God that was the Jewish vocation. But what Jesus encountered at Sepphoris was something different, something bordering on the obsessive, as though the very act of separating from the rest of the world was becoming a form of worship. The priestly classes of Sepphoris were also rich and aristocratic.

Sepphoris was quite possibly a base for the extended family of Herod Antipas, the Tetrarch of Galilee. His family comprised what almost amounted to a political party, certainly a pro-Roman pressure group. They were called Herodians, and the Gospels mention them as among the enemies of Jesus. Eric Meyers believes that Jesus may have come across the royal family of Herod Antipas in Sepphoris, parading in the streets, showing off their wealth while claiming to live lives of perfect Jewish propriety. And this was all under the protection of Roman power, Roman military strength. Though the nearest large force was far away in Syria, everyone knew that Herod Antipas, like his father, ruled only because it suited his Roman overlords. He was their vassal, in spite of his royal pretensions. Visits to Sepphoris, perhaps from childhood, would have established in the mind of the young Jesus a sinister connection between the priestly obsession with ritual purity, Roman influence and a wealthy lifestyle, which was a blatant contrast to the hard lives of the rural poor, for whom there was no opportunity to dissolve away death and contagion in the waters of a ritual bath.

The plight of the poor

The plight of the poor must have been a significant factor in Jesus' formative years. Galilee was a fertile and productive land, and there should have been enough for everyone. But Jesus' stories reflect a wide gap between rich and poor: a world of high unemployment, debt, absentee landlords milking their estates for profits, and paying low wages to their workers. The peasants of Galilee were forced to pay high taxes – between 30 and 40 per cent of their income. If harvests were poor, the peasants could all too easily fall into debt, and then have to sell what little land they had to clear their debts. Some would have tried to find employment; others would have made for the hills and a life of crime. Herod Antipas was aware of the problems of the poor and actually invited those who had lost land to come to Sepphoris for free housing and a chance to reacquire some farming land. Not many did, which may point to the fact that life, though hard, had not reached desperation point.

On the other hand, Josephus tells us that banditry was rife both in Galilee and Judea. The landscape of Palestine offered excellent shelter for rebel and bandit groups. The wilderness of Judea was an inaccessible hiding place. It was on the desert road from Jerusalem to Jericho that the traveller was mugged by thieves in Jesus' story of the Good Samaritan. In Galilee there were networks of caves in the cliffs above the Sea of Galilee that were known to have provided refuge for past generations of Jewish rebels. Josephus had no time for bandits, whom he blames for the instability that led to the eventual invasion by Rome and the destruction of Jerusalem and its temple. But he was aware that some of those suffering economic hardship in the decades that led up to the war had sympathy for the outlaws, who became popular heroes. One, Eleazar ben Dinai, was celebrated as a kind of Robin Hood character. The Gospels tell of the bandit Barabbas, who was held on capital charges at the same time as Jesus and was released by popular acclaim. In AD 6, when Jesus was a boy of nearly twelve (just before Luke has him going to the temple), a census was called for the purposes of tax assessment. This sparked a revolt led by a Galilean called Judas, whose aim was to overthrow the Roman yoke and restore Jewish independence. The revolt lasted for several years. When it was finally put down, 2,000 of the rebels were crucified.

But the suppression did not remove the sources of unrest, nor the underlying desire for things to change. Although the Jews had experienced 500 years of subordination to foreign powers, with only a relatively brief spell of genuine independence within memory, subjection was a deeply unnatural state. After all, God had given the land to the Jews and had promised to protect it if they were faithful to him. Subjection to foreign powers could only ever be a punishment or a discipline, an anomaly to be corrected in God's good time. The Jews looked back to the priestly kingdom that they had enjoyed under their own Hasmonean dynasty, and they looked forward to deliverance, which they hoped would come soon. Most believed that somehow and in some way God would intervene to save his people. There would be a Messiah. There would be salvation.

Although Rome did not rule Galilee directly, it was generally within Roman interests for estates to become larger and more productive and for individual smallholders to be absorbed into a system that could be controlled more easily from the top down. One of Herod Antipas' motives for building Sepphoris and

A reconstruction of the Nativity scene.

The wise men cross the desert with their guide.

A computer reconstruction of Bethlehem.

A Bethlehem street scene.

A dramatic reconstruction of Jesus' baptism in the River Jordan.

Liron Levo as Jesus standing by the Sea of Galilee.

A replica of a first-century boat, that Jesus and his disciples would have used, on the Sea of Galilee.

A first-century scene at the Nazareth Village Project.

Children in first-century costume at the Nazareth Village Project.

Jeremy Bowen in the ruins of Sepphoris.

A computer reconstruction of Caesarea.

Caesarea.

Jerusalem as it would have been in the time of Jesus.

Jerusalem as it is today.

Tiberias was no doubt to provide work, but the work involved accepting the institutions of an alien culture. The peasants of Galilee may not have welcomed the palaces and colonnades, the 'fast food' shops and gymnasia.

Jesus himself is utterly scathing about Herod Antipas, describing him as 'that fox' (Luke 13:32) and mocking his love of fine palaces and soft, expensive clothing (Matthew 11:8). But it is clear from the Gospels that Jesus did not seek a direct confrontation with the powerful. As a preacher and healer he would have stayed out of the towns and cities, addressing his message to villagers. It was as though he realised that political confrontation, even if it was in the name of God, would not solve the problem. Something was wrong with the relationship between God and his people, which went to the very roots.

If we imagine Jesus in his early manhood weighing up the mood of his time, developing an awareness of the reality of God, and a dawning sense of his own vocation, where would he look outside himself for inspiration? If he already harboured a suspicion that there was corruption at the heart of Jewish life, what sources of reform and renewal were there?

Was there a purification that would take away not only ritual impurity, but the contagion of fear, faithlessness, powerlessness and a compromised conscience? If Jesus rejected the option of terrorism that had inspired rebels like Judas, where else was he to look?

Alternative groups

Jesus might have been attracted to a group that Josephus joined for a time, the Essenes. They were a religious group who lived communally in towns and villages all over Palestine, practising a simple lifestyle based on a strict adherence to the Jewish law.

They were rather like monks – full members of the community practised celibacy. In 1947 an ancient library belonging to the sect was discovered at Qumran by the Dead Sea and, sub-sequently, the desert monastery where a large number of them lived. Their writings show that they rejected the Jerusalem temple, and saw themselves as an alternative sacred community with their own holy calendar and rituals. Jesus may have come across the Essenes. He shared their distrust of the Jerusalem temple and he would, like them, eventually found a communal movement concerned with the renewal of Israel. But there is no evidence that they influenced him directly. Jewish festivals are based on a lunar calendar, but the Essenes worked to a calendar based on the sun. The Essenes were driven by the need to maintain the strictest ritual purity. We know that communal meals played an important part in their life and that they took the greatest possible care to exclude any pollution of the food or the vessels of preparation. Though Jesus may have had contacts with Essenes, there is no evidence that he ever joined them or felt any great sympathy for their rigorous lifestyle.

John the Baptist

Much more important and formative for Jesus was John the Baptist, and the Gospels and Josephus both tell of John's career. He was an ascetic prophet who lived rough in the wilderness and eventually fell foul of Herod Antipas. It is possible that John might have trained for his extreme life with the Essenes, though by the time Jesus encountered him he was independent, a lone figure of towering moral strength. John was an eloquent preacher, who reminded people of the early prophets of ancient times. Not only was he passionate for God, he was indignant in God's name about social injustice. His desert lifestyle and readiness to challenge authority was in the tradition of the prophet Elijah, who had confronted the idolatry of King Ahab and his wife Jezebel. Luke is unique in telling us that John belonged to a priestly family, but perhaps like many of Luke's attractive explanations this is less than likely to be true. John believed that the corruption of priestly power had gone so far that the whole system was about to collapse. God himself would intervene and rule over his people directly. John called on people urgently to turn away from sin, and seek purification by submitting themselves to baptism in the waters of the River Jordan. He announced his baptism as a one-off event. No more could people rely on their Jewish lineage for salvation. No more could they safeguard that lineage by endless rituals of purification to which the poor had no access. God was about to purge his people in fire and judgement. Before the judgement fell there was one last chance to be forgiven and saved. Baptism in the Jordan was the way God was creating a new people, who would be preserved on the day of disaster. Baptism was a kind of re-birth, a redemption.

John's message was wholly new in the context of Judaism. His 'baptism' was so radical in its implications that he became known as 'the Baptiser'. His message went to the roots of Jewish identity, suggesting that in God's eyes, to be born a Jew, even to live as a pure Jew, was simply not enough. His baptism of repentance bypassed the temple and the priestly system altogether. Forgiveness came from confession of sins and immersion in water.

John's message spread like wildfire. The Gospels suggest something of his charisma, but it is Josephus who provides independent evidence of his influence, writing about him at much greater length than the brief reference he makes to Jesus. This reflects the fact that John, in spite of his hermit lifestyle, was a figure of public importance, who laid down an unmistakable challenge to the authorities. Josephus would have been astonished to discover that, of the two, it was Jesus who changed the course of human history. At the time, John's contribution to Jewish life seemed much more significant. His impact on the politics of Galilee is reported by the Gospels and by Josephus, though they give very different accounts of how John came to be arrested and executed by Herod Antipas. The Gospels suggest it was because Herod had made an improper marriage, but Josephus implies that John had more revolutionary intentions. The abrupt and violent ending of John the Baptist's career may have been another reason why Jesus chose to avoid direct confrontation while he was teaching and healing in Herod's territory.

John could have used a number of different locations along the banks of the Jordan for his baptisms. It is only recently that a possible site has been unearthed on what is now the Jordanian side of the Jordan. This was a no-go area during the conflict between Israel and Jordan because the area was heavily mined. But since the 1994 peace agreement, archaeologists have unearthed the foundations and remains of a number of monastery churches that date from the third century AD. Intriguingly, in the precincts of the monasteries are what look like large pools, big enough for crowds of pilgrims either to be baptised or to re-live the experience of baptism in some way. It is a bit of a long shot, but it is possible that local memory preserved the fact that this was a site used by John, and that the churches were built here to commemorate the fact.

The baptism of Jesus

The Gospels are unanimous that Jesus submitted himself to John's baptism and there is little reason to doubt their evidence. As Jesus' reputation grew it must have been difficult for Christians to accept that he had once been John's spiritual inferior, and we can see, especially in Matthew's and John's accounts of the baptism, how they struggled to reconcile their belief in Jesus as Messiah with the facts of the tradition they had received. It says something for the integrity of the writers that they kept the facts, however awkwardly they sit with what they came to believe about Jesus as 'the one who', as John himself had prophesied, 'was to come'. The Gospels imply that Jesus was for some time one of John's disciples, and that he even assisted with the baptism rituals. In John's Gospel Jesus and John divide up the task with Jesus baptising in the Judean countryside (not in Galilee at all) and John the Baptist to the north in Samaria. John was never quite certain that Jesus was the promised one. The Gospels report him sending Jesus a message from Herod's prison asking him, 'Are you the one who is to come, or are we to wait for another?' (Matthew 11:2).

The most important thing about Jesus' baptism is that it was the moment when his own vocation seems to have crystallised. He had a strong sense of being filled with the Holy Spirit, and called by God into a relationship of special intimacy. The Gospel writers claim that a heavenly voice spoke to him and called him 'beloved son'. In Judaism the testimony of a heavenly voice is a sign of special holiness. The baptism was a turning point, but it did not at this stage lead to any public announcement of Jesus' mission. Instead, the Gospels tell us, Jesus withdrew from society and went into the wilderness.

Jesus in the wilderness

The Judean desert is to the east of the hill country of Judea as it descends to the Dead Sea. It is a fantastic region of cliffs and rocks and caves, almost barren of vegetation, scorching hot by day and cool by night. Even after 2,000 years, the stillness and

47

silence is majestic. The attraction of the desert goes back to the roots of Israel's faith. It was in the desert of Sinai that Moses met God manifested in the burning bush. It was during their wanderings in the Sinai desert that God bound his people to himself in the covenant of the Ten Commandments, a covenant that was often seen as a kind of marriage between God and Israel. It is not surprising that the desert came to be seen as a place of intimacy with God, a place of renewal and discernment where the will of God could reveal itself in the fiery crucible of temptation.

Jesus went into the desert for forty days and forty nights. This is a traditional number. The Israelites wandered in the wilderness for forty years. Elijah was forty days and forty nights in the wilderness before he came to Horeb, the mount of God. Forty days is about as long as a human being can go without food. Jesus must have had water to drink or else he would have died of dehydration. Travellers to the desert today need to take water with them even if they are only going for a few hours. Dehydration can strike quickly in the dry, relentless heat.

The Gospels give three versions of Jesus' time in the desert. The shortest is Mark's, which compresses the experience into a few bare sentences (Mark 1:12–14). He simply reports that Jesus was tempted by Satan, that he was with the wild beasts, and that the angels came and looked after him. Matthew and Luke have longer versions. Whether Jesus himself passed on an account of what happened to him or whether early Christian preachers and teachers reflected on what must have happened as Jesus faced the reality of his vocation, we do not know. The temptation stories show us Jesus trying to discover what God wants of him. The figure of Satan in these stories is here a kind of spiritual trainer, not the horned and tailed bogey-man of later Christian imagination. Satan's job is to provoke Jesus and to test his worth, by forcing him to choose from a range of ways of living out his vocation.

All the strategies Satan presents to Jesus have a place in Jewish Scripture and tradition and none of them is obviously wrong. The first temptation was for Jesus to produce miraculous bread from the stones of the desert (Matthew 4:3-4; Luke 4:3-4). Nothing wrong with that; God had rained manna from heaven on the Israelites. In a world where a bad harvest could lead to hunger, the power to feed people would have been ample proof of Jesus' vocation. However, Jesus rejected this temptation. The kind of renewal he hoped for involved more than an improvement in people's material hopes. Bread was not enough. Another suggestion from Satan was to stage a spectacular miracle, to show once and for all that he was the chosen one of God (Matthew 4:5-6; Luke 4:9-12). This too Jesus rejected; it was an attempt to force God's hand, to put God to the test.

Yet another possible invitation from Satan was for Jesus to seek to become a ruler (Matthew 4:8-9; Luke 4:5-8). This would fulfil Israel's hopes about the Messiah. The psalms looked forward to the day when God's anointed one would rule the nations with a rod of iron. Yet again, Jesus rejected this invitation as a temptation to idolatry. Whatever God's will for him was, it could not be in seeking to surpass Herod, or even Caesar, in power or dignity.

After three attempts, Satan runs out of options and Jesus is able to dismiss him. By standing up to Satan as an adversary Jesus shows he has mastery of himself, that his deepest trust is in God. From now on his way will be the way of dependence. The Son, to be a true Son, must trust the Father to reveal his will.

Later on, Jesus did, apparently, perform miracles. He was believed to have presided over miraculous meals at which bread multiplied in the hands of those who distributed it. But perhaps there would not have been any stories about feeding miracles in the Gospels if he had previously given in to the temptation to put his own needs first.

Whatever we make of the temptation stories, the Jesus who emerges from the desert clearly had a confidence and conviction about him that was even more compelling than that of John, who was by now confined to prison. At about the age of thirty Jesus returns to Galilee announcing: 'The time is fulfilled, and the kingdom of God has come near; repent, and believe in the good news' (Mark 1:15).

3

ENEMIES AND FRIENDS

So Jesus appears in Galilee. After thirty years of anonymity he suddenly becomes known as a preacher. After a period as John the Baptist's apprentice he emerges in his own right. Jesus stops baptising people. John's Gospel rather fudges the issue about whether Jesus actually did conduct baptisms. There is a contradiction between John 3:22, which describes him baptising in Judea, and John 4:2, which says that only his disciples baptised. Anyway, for the time being baptisms stopped and would not start again until his disciples revived the practice after Jesus' death. The essence of the message of Jesus is that the kingdom of God has drawn near. He keeps John's urgency, but there is less of the solemnity and threat of judgement. Those who hear are to repent and believe, to receive the coming kingdom with joy. His preaching plays less on people's fears than on their hopes and dreams.

Jesus' message stirred things up – not on the scale that John the Baptist's message had, but then Jesus was never such an obviously impressive or extreme figure as John. He did not wear distinctive clothing. He did not have the romance of the desert about him. He was clearly not a fan of Herod Antipas, but he did not challenge the authorities directly. He avoided trouble rather than confronting it, and seemed to have acquired effective techniques of escaping if danger beckoned. Most of the time Jesus was content to wander among the villages and hamlets of the coast of the Sea of Galilee, preaching the good news among the poor and unimportant.

It is difficult for us to know quite how his message was heard. Mark says (Mark 12:37) that ordinary people heard him gladly, but it seems that his preaching was not always effective. There were plenty who did not want to know, who guessed that if they got involved with Jesus life would never be the same, and decided to steer clear of him. Did they think of him as a religious figure or a rabble rouser?

It is usual for us to make a distinction between religion and politics, but in Jesus' time this distinction would have been meaningless. The reign of God would be bound to have implications for the relationship between rulers and ruled. At the very least, it would set limits on the power of Rome to determine human destiny. While not being overtly revolutionary, it would put question marks over the luxurious lifestyle and royal posturing of Herod Antipas and his family. It would have encouraged people to be reconciled to one another, to pay up or forgive any debts, to examine their consciences and seek forgiveness.

But it is difficult from our perspective to see why, eventually, this message would get Jesus killed.

We need to delve more deeply into the politics of the time to understand why the movement Jesus started led him to

confrontation with the rulers of his people and to death und
the Romans. We are so used to thinking of Jesus' life as a series
of almost static peaceful tableaux – the baby in the manger, the
boy preacher in the temple, the baptised young man rising from
the water, the ascetic in the desert, the teacher of sublime spiritual
truths in the sermon on the mount – that we neglect the religious
and nationalistic fervour to which his life and mission were a
response.

Jesus proclaimed the kingdom of God, but he had grown up
subject to two earthly kingdoms: that of Herod the Great and his
successors, and that of imperial Rome. Before that, there were
1,000 years of history in which the Jews struggled to realise what
God wanted of them in the Holy Land they believed he had
given them. This history shaped the Jews of Jesus' time and
shaped him. It still shapes the hopes and fears of Jews today.

The land

Looking at a map one might wonder at God's choice of location
for his holy people. The strip of land that forms biblical Israel
runs south to north between much greater land masses. Israel is
inherently vulnerable. To the north-east, Babylonia is the great
power; to the south, Egypt. Much of Israel's history was
hammered out of the conflicts that belong to the geography of
the region, conflicts that continue to this day.

David and Solomon

A thousand years before Christ was the reign of King David,
Israel's ideal and much idealised monarch, from whom, as
Matthew and Luke try to demonstrate, Jesus was descended. The
real David is an elusive figure whose conquests are not mentioned

in historical records apart from the Old Testament histories. He was also a much more frail figure than he was sometimes remembered as being: capable of betrayal, deceit and shabby dealing, which are all spelt out without mercy in Israel's historical books. It's as though in Israel's history the ideal is always intertwined with a tragic sense that even the most gifted people cannot live up to what is expected of them. David's history has a legendary flavour to it, so it is difficult to determine how much of his story is true. It was certainly believed that he had carved out a great empire. The extent of this empire varies in different records, but one of the most frequent estimates is that it stretched as far as Dan in the north and Beersheba to the south. Dan is nearly thirty miles north of the Sea of Galilee deep into present-day Syria. Beersheba is in the south of Judea near the southern desert of the Negev. David made Jerusalem his capital and prepared the way for the building of the temple, a sanctuary for the ark of the covenant. When Jews looked back to David they saw their nation state as they believed it should be, united under God, independent of foreign influence, extending over the territory of the whole of the twelve tribes of Israel, focused on the holy city of Jerusalem.

According to the Old Testament histories, it was David's successor, Solomon, who brought this ideal monarchy to the pinnacle of its success. Famed for his wisdom, Solomon crowned David's achievements by building the temple. He also took on an international role, forging trading alliances with neighbouring states and building up a merchant fleet of ships. He married magnificently – and often; wealth poured into Jerusalem. But his very success contained within it the seeds of his destruction. Solomon was seduced by his grandeur. To achieve his ambitions he rode rough-shod over the rights of his people and pressed them into forced labour. He abandoned his loyalty to God alone and began to worship foreign deities. In spite of their weaknesses, though, David and Solomon were powerful legendary figures in Jewish imagination. The followers of Jesus came to see him as great David's even greater son, and Jesus himself is reported as having hinted of himself that 'something greater than Solomon is here' (Matthew 12:42; Luke 11:31).

The two kingdoms

On the death of Solomon rebellion broke out, which led to the division of the kingdom. There were now two kingdoms, of Israel and Judah, precariously lodged between the greater and more powerful nations to the north and south. Both kingdoms were, inevitably, weakened by having been separated.

The independence of the northern kingdom of Israel lasted for nearly two hundred years, but then the rising power of Assyria cast a shadow over its future. The Assyrian empire centred around the city of Nineveh on the River Tigris. Today, Assyria itself is northern Iraq. In Israel, the prophets of the north, Elijah, Amos and Hosea, railed against idolatry and social injustice. As the threat of Assyria came nearer, the prophets interpreted the impending catastrophe as a judgement from God that could be averted if the nation returned to righteous ways. But there was very little that could be done to save Israel. Even if the kingdom had become a nation of exceptional virtue, it would not have stopped the expansionist monarch Tiglath-Pileser III from wanting control in the region. In the event he took tribute from Israel and subjected the region to Assyrian control, but it was not until after his death that Israel was invaded and defeated in 722 BC. About 27,000 citizens of the leading families of Israel were exiled, and exiles from other parts of the empire were settled on Israel's soil. It was a disastrous end to a dream of freedom, but the legacy of the prophets who had boldly challenged the nation's rulers was remembered. When John the Baptist arrived on the scene in the days of Herod the Great, preaching repentance, he resembled the Elijah of popular imagination who had stood up to King Ahab and his wife, the scheming Jezebel. Jesus himself was taken by some to be a reappearance of Elijah.

The southern kingdom of Judah lasted for another 164 years. It survived threats from Assyria, and even an invasion, without succumbing. The prophet Isaiah helped the royal house to stand firm. In 622–1 BC, King Josiah led a religious reformation after a book of the law was found in the Jerusalem temple. He cleansed the land of foreign cults and recalled the people to their ancestral faith. However, trouble was at hand from both the south and the north. Josiah was killed by an adventurous king of Egypt, and his son and heir was taken to Egypt as a hostage. The real danger, though, was to come from the east, from the rising power of Babylon.

Exile

This time there was no escape, but it took the people of Judah a while to take that in. Under a succession of monarchs they tried to play power-politics by forging temporary alliances with other small states, aided by Egypt. But these alliances only served to destabilise the situation even more. The prophet Jeremiah advised surrender and got persecuted for his pains. In 597 the Babylonians intervened and King Jehoiachin and the cream of Judah's society were removed and forced to live in Babylonia. A new king, Zedekiah, was appointed as a puppet of Babylon, but the people of Judah still struggled against the inevitable, hatching new plots against Babylon until the greater power ran out of patience. In 586 Jerusalem was captured and burnt, and the temple was destroyed. There was then another forced migration to Babylonia. This was the end of independence for the kingdom of Judah for more than 300 years.

The exile was an important spiritual experience for the people of Judah. They discovered that it was possible to live a life of faith in God even in an unclean land, that the distinctive observances of the Sabbath and the purity laws helped to keep their identity intact. The exile began the process by which the Jews became a people of the book. Though there were no synagogues as such at this time, the exiles began to discover that it was possible to pray and study the law in the absence of the temple and its rituals. It was the beginning of another kind of Judaism. The prophets of the exile looked forward to a return to the land and a restoration of pure worship in a renewed temple. Some of them even began to preach that Judaism had a mission to bring enlightenment to the other nations. These new tendencies were the seeds of the spiritualising of Judaism that would influence the Pharisees, the Essenes, and Jesus himself.

In spite of the prophets' hopes, independence was not regained for many years. From being under the control of Babylon, Palestine was taken over by the Persian empire. The Persians had a different policy from that of the Babylonians and permitted the exiles to return. The temple was rebuilt from 520 onwards and refocused Jewish life around the sacrificial system. After the rule of Persia, Judah came under Egyptian influence, and was later incorporated into the empire of the Syrian Seleucid kings.

The desecration of the temple

One of the Seleucid kings, Antiochus Epiphanes (175–63), was an ardent admirer of Hellenism, the Greek way of life introduced into the Middle East in the wake of the conquests of Alexander the Great. He tried to impose Hellenistic culture on the Jews, with an appalling lack of sensitivity to their traditional beliefs. Some Jews supported him and there were conflicts between those who saw no contradiction between Judaism and Hellenism, and those for whom Greek ways were anathema. As Antiochus' policies took a grip, Jerusalem became virtually a pagan city, the temple was plundered, and at that point the more conservative Jews rose up in revolt. Severe reprisals followed. Antiochus Epiphanes decided that his policies had not gone far enough. It was no use aiming for an accommodation between Judaism and Hellenism, the Jewish religion must be exterminated. All the distinctive marks of Jewishness – the Sabbath, the food laws, circumcision and the reading of the law – all this must be abolished on pain of death. Altars were set up to pagan gods, Jews were forced to eat pigs' flesh, and the temple itself was desecrated with an image of Zeus, probably bearing the features of Antiochus Epiphanes himself. As a final touch, sacrificed pig was offered to the image.

It was impossible for self-respecting Jews to live under these conditions, though those in charge of the temple under the Syrians shamefully submitted to the new regime. But many others refused, and when attempts were made to compel them to eat pork, they chose death instead. Revolt broke out when an elderly priest, Mattathias, and his five sons defied the agents of Antiochus by killing a Jew prepared to make the idolatrous sacrifice. The priest and his family fled to the wilderness, where they were joined by other deeply religious Jews who were devoted to the law, and were prepared to fight to the death in defence of their traditions. The Jewish revolt took the form of guerrilla warfare against the Syrians. Groups of rebels would descend on villages, destroy the pagan altars, circumcise the boys, and murder those who had compromised their faith by offering sacrifices to idols. Under their leader, Judas Maccabaeus, the rebels succeeded in destroying Syrian forces sent to suppress the revolution. His army marched on Jerusalem and liberated both city and temple. The temple was rededicated in December 164 BC. This was the origin of the Jewish feast of Hanukkah, which coincides with Christmas. Full independence was achieved some twenty years later. From 142 to 63 BC, the Jews lived as God's holy people, free from foreign domination, in their own holy land.

The Hasmonean monarchy

The independent kingdom was ruled over by a succession of High Priests, descendants of the original Maccabees. Their role was to combine religious and secular leadership. Later rulers took the title 'king' in addition to that of High Priest. The Hasmonean monarchs extended the boundaries of Israel and forcibly converted some of their neighbours. Where they could, they imposed taxes, with the result that wealth began to flow into the country. Inevitably, the High Priest and his family began to accumulate wealth and to enjoy a more and more affluent lifestyle. This attracted criticism from the pious. By the end of the second century BC, there were clear divisions between those who, in general, supported the hereditary priesthood, and those who believed that even the priesthood and the temple should come under the law. The Sadducees were the party who represented the interests of the High Priest and the governing classes. They were traditionalists in their understanding of the law and they held to the belief that there is no afterlife. The Pharisees, on the other hand, were not drawn from the governing classes. Many of them had given moral and spiritual support to the rebels. They had missionary zeal; they wanted to popularise the

Jewish law and make it more accessible to ordinary people. They wanted people to understand the requirements of purity not only through the rituals of the temple, but through personal faith and practice.

The rise of Rome

Jewish independence lasted until the middle of the first century BC when Palestine became engulfed in the adventures and conflicts of another world power, Rome. Following the assassination of Julius Caesar, the Roman empire was riven by civil war. In 63 BC the Roman warlord Pompey laid claim to Judea. Arriving in Jerusalem he horrified the Jews by entering the temple to see what fascinating or obscene image really lurked inside the holy of holies. However, he was disappointed to discover there really was nothing there. He was later commended by his fellow-countrymen for not looting the temple; but when he was killed some years later in Egypt, a number of Jews interpreted his death as a divine punishment for having entered the holy of holies.

There was nothing much the Jews could do, however, about the power of Rome. The most they could manage was the kind of semi-independence achieved by Herod the Great. It was a Hasmonean ruler who appointed one of Herod's great-grandfathers to rule the Idumean people who lived in the south of Palestine. The Herodians were successful political operators and eventually Herod's father got himself Roman citizenship and was appointed procurator of Judea. His son, Herod, started his political career as governor of Galilee in 47 BC. He played his hand there cleverly, rounding up and executing local bandits with such zealous brutality that he was summoned to give account of his actions to the Jewish court in Jerusalem. He was sentenced to death but quickly escaped, gathered support in Lebanon and

Samaria, and prepared to launch an attack on the Holy City itself. He was persuaded to desist, but his bold actions made Rome take notice of him. Here was an intelligent bully who would stand no nonsense, even from the notoriously querulous Jews. Ten years later he gained Roman support to lay siege to Jerusalem, fighting for the city street by street until he had control. He was almost too successful in his efforts to subdue it and had to bribe the Roman soldiers at the last minute not to destroy both city and temple.

Herod the Great and his successors

So began the bloody, scandalous, but effective reign of Herod the Great, towards the end of which Jesus was born. The unity Herod had imposed on Palestine fell apart at his death, and Jewish identity was traumatised by the loss of real independence in Judea. The temple was compromised, the countryside was full of crime and violence, and the undying hope that God would set his people free gave a mandate to rebels and crackpots alike to announce the arrival of salvation. The land we now call Israel was a cauldron of conflicting loyalties and desperate, impossible dreams.

Judea remained the heart of the country with its sacred and sophisticated capital in Jerusalem. Galilee in the north was the gateway to the world beyond Judaism. Between Galilee and Judea was the country of Samaria, inhabited by people who believed they were Jews but who were not accepted as such by other Jews.

At the time of Jesus, the Roman presence in the area was located in the coastal town of Caesarea where Herod had built a magnificent new harbour. It was one of the biggest in the Mediterranean, protected by vast stone breakwaters, the remains of which can still be seen from the air. The Roman governors lived here, protected by a cavalry cohort and five infantry cohorts, a total of about 3,000 men. None of them, of course, were Jewish. The Jews were exempt from military service, largely because they would have been unable to keep the food laws or the Sabbath, and so were not thought to be worth the hassle involved in drafting them into the army. The consequence was that all Roman soldiers were regarded as foreign and unclean by the Jews. There was not the remotest sympathy between rulers and ruled. It was Romans from Caesarea who patrolled Judea after its annexation. Soldiers were sent from Caesarea to Jerusalem at times of tension, particularly when the city was crammed at Passover and Jewish nationalist fervour ran high. The Romans were not and could not be loved, and they knew it.

There was less of an obvious Roman presence in Galilee. Herod the Great could not command Roman forces, but he had his own army that he organised on the Roman model. He kept troops in one of his cities, Sebaste in Samaria, halfway between Judea and Galilee. He had others near Mount Carmel who could get to Galilee quickly if there was any trouble. Galilee saw what Roman military power could do during the riots after the death of Herod, when extra troops were rushed in from Syria to put down the insurrection and burn Sepphoris. After the annexation of Judea, Herod Antipas built up his troops to defend his new territory of Galilee and Perea, while knowing that, at a last resort, he too could call on the Romans.

The shadow of the temple

Jesus became a famous preacher and healer in the shadow of Herod the Great's son and the greater shadow of Roman influence and power. The temple was the place where both shadows met. The Romans knew nothing of Jesus until the last few days of his life, but he would have been aware of them from infancy. His awareness would have included the fact that the temple in Jerusalem, the centre and focus of Jewish identity, owed its splendour to the determination of Herod to make it an acclaimed monument. In the end it was also only available for Jews to worship in because the Romans controlled the priestly families who ran it. It was Roman power that allowed the Jews access. The Jews might have appeared free to worship their God, but it was freedom bought at a price. The temple was vulnerable, as it always had been. Destroyed by the Babylonians, gradually and painfully restored by the returning exiles, and then desecrated first as a deliberate act by Antiochus Epiphanes, and more recently, casually, by the Roman general Pompey, the temple was always vulnerable. Some forty years after the crucifixion that vulnerability was again, and finally, exposed. In AD 70 the Romans, provoked beyond endurance by the Jews, marched into Jerusalem, burnt city and temple to the ground, and carried the temple treasures back to Rome. Scenes from the final conquest, including the capture of the sacred menorah, are depicted on the inside of the triumphal arch of Titus in Rome.

That was the final end of the temple, the temple cult, the priests, the round of prayers and sacrifices on which Israel's relationship with God had depended. It was also the end of the High Priesthood, the party of the Sadducees who supported them, and the Essenes who opposed them. All disappeared from history as a consequence of the great revolt. Judaism was convulsed by the final loss of the temple. The form of Judaism that survived was that of the Pharisees, who developed their own distinctive religious approach into the Rabbinic Judaism that still flourishes today.

Since AD 70 the site on which the temple stood has been a battleground. In the seventh century the first great monument of Islam was built, the Dome of the Rock, right on top of the rocky mound built up by Herod. This was not a mosque as such – more a visible symbol to both Christians and Jews of the religious superiority of Islam. The crusaders took the area into Christian control and turned the Dome into a church. It became Muslim again under the Turks and is still under Muslim control. But in 1967, during the Six Day War, Israel captured the Old City of Jerusalem and the last remaining wall of Herod's temple was restored to Jewish oversight. This is the western or 'wailing' wall where Jews from all over the globe come to pray. For some Jews the present arrangement is not enough; they want the whole site of the temple mount restored to Jewish control. A few hotheads even dream of rebuilding the temple, though it is impossible to imagine restoring the place into the bloody abattoir it must once have resembled.

When we see how the Jewish dream of independence and control still has power to ignite nationalist and religious passions, it does not take much imagination to see how the plight of the Jews under the Herodians and the Romans built up dreams of freedom in the first century. At the end of the Six Day War in 1967, there were fervent Jews who were so excited at their victory over the Arabs that they really believed the Messiah was about to arrive. With each shift in the balance of power in first-century Palestine, there were outbreaks of the same excitement, the gleam of hope that God's people would finally see God's kingdom in God's own Holy Land.

Messiah

Many Jews, then as now, hoped for a 'Messiah'. The word 'Messiah' simply means 'anointed one' and it could be used of those anointed for office as High Priest or king. Some Jewish literature of around the time of Jesus uses the term to apply to a superhuman or idealised figure appointed by God to liberate his people. Therefore 'Messiah' could mean many things, then as now. Some thought the Messiah would be a warrior; some assumed he would lead a supernatural battle against evil; some thought he would rule on earth; and others believed that he would reign for a period of time and then hand his rule over to God. The Dead Sea scrolls show that some at least of the Essenes hoped for two Messiahs: a royal one and a priestly one. There are Jewish writings, like the book of Daniel, that speak of a promised figure in different terms, as a 'Son of Man'. Jesus used this term of himself, with devastating consequences. Other Jews expected God to intervene directly without the need for a human or superhuman agent.

Jesus, in his preaching and in his person, tapped into these dreams about coming Messiahs and God's intervention, and that was the secret of his popularity. Of course people wondered if he was the Messiah. They had speculated about Judas the Galilean who ended up crucified with his 2,000 followers; likewise, they had wondered about John the Baptist, who had been executed in Herod's jail. Jesus was bound to be a focus for hopes of national restoration.

But Jesus was different from Judas the Galilean and John the Baptist. He had no army and never tried to raise one. He was not a terrorist. Even if he could have made the claim to have come from the royal house of David, he had not the slightest chance of any claim to royal status being accepted. He did not, at least at the beginning of his career as a preacher, court danger or death. Jesus' strategy for the kingdom was quite different. He took a long step backwards from the cities and the bandit strongholds and started his revolution among fishermen.

Capernaum

Jesus started gathering support from the fishermen of Galilee because he was thrown out of Nazareth. Luke, as we have already seen, describes him virtually announcing himself as the Messiah in the synagogue at Nazareth (Luke 4:16 ff). Whether this happened precisely as Luke tells it or not, Jesus came to the conclusion that his message was not welcome in his home town and he took to the coast, about thirty miles away. The Sea of Galilee is an inland lake fed from the northern stretch of the Jordan, which itself is fed from rivers that run down from the mountains of Syria. The southern end of the lake tapers into the Jordan again. The valley of the Jordan makes a natural border, winding its way south as the land drops dramatically to the plains of Moab and the Dead Sea. Capernaum was a small fishing village at the northern end of the lake. Jesus' first followers lived here. Their names were Simon, Andrew, James and John.

In 1985 a drought in Galilee caused extra demand from farmers for water, and the Israeli water system drew heavily on the reserves in the lake. Because there was so little rain to replenish the lake, the water level dropped lower than in living memory. This exposed an astonishing relic. Buried in the mud were the water-logged remains of a wooden fishing boat, about 27 feet long and 7½ feet wide. Coins and pottery found in the mud, and radio-carbon testing of the wood, show that the boat must date from between 40 BC and AD 40. It was quickly named 'Jesus' boat', or 'Peter's boat' (Jesus did not have one of his own). Of course, there is no reason to think it actually was a boat belonging to one of Jesus' disciples, but it just *could* be – and it certainly comes from the right time and place. Peter's boat was big enough to carry Jesus and all the disciples across the lake. It had room for several men to work the wide nets and drag them ashore.

Disciples

Jesus began with fishermen, but then he recruited men from other walks of life. The Gospels are unanimous in saying that there were twelve who were specially called. The number twelve would have reminded people of the twelve tribes of Israel, and so might have suggested that Jesus was forming a new community. It was certainly a different community. Matthew was a tax collector, and would have been enormously unpopular. Tax collectors worked for their overlords and charged what they needed to include their own cut. Not only were they working for the enemy, they were also widely believed to be profiting from their own people. The call of Matthew is described as having happened in Capernaum, which suggests that Matthew worked for Herod Antipas, unlike the tax collector Zacchaeus, in Judea, who must have worked directly for the Romans. Capernaum was a border post between Herod Antipas' territory of Galilee and his brother Philip's region to the north-east, which was largely populated by Gentiles. There would have been plenty of opportunities to raise taxes on goods passing to and fro. Heaven knows how Matthew managed to get on with Peter, Andrew, James and John, who probably regarded him as a parasite, feeding off their hard-won profits. Another recruit was a Zealot called Simon. Josephus describes the Zealots as members of a resistance movement who fought against the Romans in the revolt that began in AD 66. The presence of a Zealot among the disciples may be an anachronism, as no one is sure whether they really existed in the time of Jesus, but given the variety of nationalistic dreamers, royal pretenders and would-be Messiahs there were in

Jesus' day, we can assume that it was someone like the later Zealots that Jesus had in his team. Then there was Judas Iscariot, who looked after the finances, and probably came from Judea.

Jesus seems to have had an especially close relationship with three of his first disciples – Simon (whom he nicknamed Peter), James, and John. Peter was regarded as his right-hand man and tradition claims that Jesus singled him out as the leader of the new community. The name Peter means 'rock', and so he was to be the rock of the new faith. Peter was essential for the mission of Jesus, not least because he provided him with his headquarters. Peter lived in Capernaum, presumably with his wife and children. He certainly had a mother-in-law, because the Gospels speak of her being healed from a fever by Jesus.

Peter's house

The fishing town of Capernaum has been extensively excavated; it was little more than a cluster of homes along the lake front. The evidence is quite strong for the site of Peter's house. There was clearly Christian devotion on this site before Queen Helena's travels in the fourth century when many more holy places were discovered. We know that Christians were living here because there are records of conflicts between Jews and Christians. A pilgrim called Egeria, towards the end of the fourth century, reported that the house of the 'prince of the apostles' had been made into a church. An excavation of the area took place a hundred years ago, and the archaeologists found the remains of a fifth-century church.

Underneath was an earlier church that had been build round the remains of a first-century house. In the rubble of the original house remnants of fishing equipment were discovered. The house clearly belonged to a fisherman, and it turned out to be one of a number of small, poorly built houses, only distinguished from those around it by the fact that the walls were plastered. Archaeologists found fragments of plaster on which simple Christian prayers had been inscribed, such as 'Lord Jesus Christ help your servant' and 'Christ have mercy'. These are testimony that the house had some significance for early Christians. It is likely that they met for worship here, and it is certainly possible that the reason this house was chosen was because local people had handed on the memory that the house had once belonged to Peter.

Today the house and the first churches built over it are invisible from the ground. A modern concrete church stands over the site, but it is just possible to imagine a group of small houses, with their light drystone walls and flimsy roofs, clustered together near the seashore. This was where Jesus started his revolutionary campaign, where he planted the seed of his kingdom on earth. Nothing about it was secret, but neither was it likely to be known to anyone who mattered. The Romans could not have cared less. And that is because, though Jesus must have disliked the foreign power and longed to see the Holy Land free, it was not the Romans who stood in the way of the kingdom of God. It was Jesus' own people, and in particular the priests.

The temple tax

The temple was seventy miles away from Capernaum, yet the temple authorities extracted tax from the poorest of fishermen and peasants. This was half a shekel per person in addition to the rest of their tax burden. A delightful 'magical' story from the Gospels describes what happened when the temple tax collectors came to Capernaum and interrogated Peter about whether Jesus was in the habit of paying up. Peter replied that he did, but the answer was not as simple as that. In conversation with Peter afterwards, Jesus posed a rhetorical question about whether kings claimed tribute from their heirs or from their subjects. Peter replied that kings would always claim tribute from their subjects. They would not disadvantage their own families. Jesus replied enigmatically to this, 'Then the children are free'. He is implying that 'the children', the true sons and daughters of Israel, the heirs of the temple, should not be expected to pay tribute. They are beneficiaries of the temple and they are not to be exploited by the temple. The conclusion of the story is almost farcical. So as not to cause offence, Jesus will pay the temple tax and will pay Peter's too. Jesus tells Peter to go and cast a line into the sea and take the first fish that comes up. In its mouth will be a coin, a whole shekel which will pay for the two of them (Matthew 17:24–7).

This little story is rarely read in public, no doubt because the compilers of lectionaries do not want to encourage an irresponsible attitude towards personal taxation. There have been one or two strained efforts to see Jesus' command to Peter to find the coin in the fish's mouth as an instruction to continue with his work as a fisherman so that he will earn enough to pay the tax without difficulty. But the story is in such a light spirit that this tedious interpretation ruins it. No, the point of the story is to poke fun at the temple, to show how its demands can and should be treated casually by those who are its true heirs. The kingdom of God has come and the children will soon be free. Jesus is shaking the foundations of the whole sacred world of Jewish tradition with a joke about paying the mandatory temple tax with a coin spat from a dead fish's mouth.

Jesus never forgot either the reach or the power of the Jewish temple. The effect it had on the peasants and fishermen he preached to was not limited to taxation. Its influence extended into every aspect of their lives through the laws of purity.

Enemies

Here we have to be careful in our reading of the Gospels. They imply that among the chief enemies of Jesus were the Pharisees. The Gospels depict the Pharisees as, on the whole, a puritanical bunch, over-concerned with issues of food and drink, over-rigorous in their Sabbath observance, proud, vain and nit-picking on all sorts of minor issues. This is a bit of a travesty, for it also conceals an anachronism. We have to remember that the Gospels were written about forty years after the crucifixion, in the years leading up to and following the Jewish war against the Romans when the temple was finally destroyed. By that time, the influence of the Pharisees as a party was on the increase; soon they would be the only major surviving force in Judaism. The Gospel writers, who may not have had a very clear grasp on the different parties in Judaism earlier in the century, tend to attribute attitudes to the Pharisees that may not have belonged to them at the time of Jesus. There are even some scholars who think it unlikely that there were any Pharisees at all in Galilee at the time of Jesus! Whether there were or not, it was not the Pharisees as a group who were Jesus' real target. In fact, he shared a great deal with them. He understood their kind of Judaism with its zeal for God, and its longing to express God's holiness and justice not only by outward behaviour but by a prayerful heart and a positive, generous and forgiving attitude towards others.

Jesus' targets were the priests who enforced the Jewish purity laws from the central sanctuary of the Jerusalem temple. The priesthood and the temple were controlled by the Sadducees, though there were Pharisees who also had influence. One of the great rabbis of Judaism, Simon the Righteous, once remarked that the world stands on three things: the Torah, the temple service, and deeds of loving-kindness. Many Jews believed that

71

the temple was a real visible link between earth and heaven. The regular performance of its sacrifices, carried out daily and seasonally according to ritual law, played a key part in the smooth running of the world, providing order and continuity for Jew and non-Jew alike. The temple had a kind of cosmic significance. It was a time ship. When the High Priest stood before God in the temple, he represented all of Israel and all of humanity. Through the temple service came cosmic order and the setting right of human sin.

All this is clear from Jewish writings from before and after the time of Jesus. Even those who criticised the temple, like the Essenes, imagined alternatives that would provide what the temple provided in a different way. Even the Pharisees, who were often ambiguous about the temple, cared enormously about ritual order. They wanted to domesticate the ritual and make it more a part of everyday life, but they assumed by doing this they were still providing the link between earth and heaven that the temple existed to ensure.

The Gospels mention other groups who opposed Jesus. Among them were lawyers and scribes. It is difficult to identify precisely who the lawyers were. The term simply seems to stand for those members of the Jewish ruling classes with whom Jesus came into conflict! No doubt they were literate officials of some sort, linked to the Sadducees and to the temple system. More can be said of the scribes. Scribes were valued throughout the ancient world because they were highly literate, and therefore entrusted with drawing up and interpreting legal documents. In the Babylonian exiles, scribes were responsible for interpreting Scripture. Their role meant that they were seen as figures who dispensed wisdom. In the Gospels they function more or less like lawyers and are usually depicted disputing with Jesus on questions of authority and tradition.

The other group mentioned as enemies of Jesus, especially by Luke, were the Herodians, the party that supported the royal family of Herod, the Tetrarch of Galilee.

The temple service

Thanks to the efforts of a scholar from Durham University, Robert Hayward, we are able to deduce quite a lot about the worship of the Jerusalem temple. He has gathered together a wide range of descriptions and presented them in a way that forms a consistent whole. For example, an account preserved by Josephus, which may come from the third century BC, tells us that there were 1,500 priests at any one time receiving the temple tithes and administering the affairs of the temple. Where did these priests come from? They lived all over Palestine, but they were brought in by a rota to serve their period of duty in Jerusalem. It needed a lot of people to keep the services going day and night, all through the year. The constancy of worship was symbolised by the inextinguishable light on the altar, a reminder that God's glory was contained here. A Jewish observer writing about a hundred years before Christ mentions the endless supply of water that flushed away the blood of sacrifices. The divine service was conducted in silence; no one needed to give commands. The 700 ministering priests carried out their duties without any instruction being given. The High Priest wore a magnificent robe to conduct the temple service; it was embroidered with flowers and pomegranates, and from its hem hung golden bells. He wore a breastplate with twelve precious stones mounted on it. His head was covered in a turban and a mitre, on which the unpronounceable name of God was engraved on a fillet of gold. The veil separating off the holy of holies was in the path of a draught, and it billowed ceaselessly backwards and forwards.

There was worship in the morning and the evening. The morning sacrifice atoned for the sins of the night; the evening sacrifice for the sins of the day. Individuals came to the temple with their offering to be sacrificed and to receive the forgiveness of sins. The temple services involved the slaughter of lambs, but they also included the offering of incense and the ritual lighting of lamps on the seven-branched lampstand. The Sabbath was a special day. The bread of the presence was provided on the golden table in the court of the priests, along with salt as a symbol of preservation and holiness. The old bread was consumed by the priests. A first-century document by a Jew living in Palestine takes up a metaphor used by Isaiah and others in describing Israel as a vine planted on Mount Zion. The vine holds together the different parts of creation, and this is the special vocation of the Jewish people. The temple, as embellished by Herod, had a complex vine decorating the entrance to the sanctuary. For the first-century writer the symbol of the vine would have been crucial to his understanding of the significance of the temple. The vine keeps God's attention on the world and the human race. For God to abandon his vine would be to abandon creation altogether.

For the temple authorities the maintenance of ritual purity was crucial for the cosmic work of the temple to be effective. But in the stressful years after the loss of Jewish independence, the purity laws came to take on a new significance: they came to be a totem of national identity. The temple authorities came to have a vested interest in emphasising the things about Judaism that made them different. Their power and prestige depended on the temple, so the temple itself had to be the most significant marker of Jewish identity. No doubt the priests took inspiration from the memories of the Maccabees and the struggle to undo the desecration of the temple under Antiochus Epiphanes. This was the clearest example in Jewish history of the unbreakable link between the temple and the affirmation of Jewishness. The rededication of the temple led directly to the revival of the nation. For this reason, the temple authorities were prepared to compromise on all kinds of issues as long as the temple service remained intact. They were rather like the leaders of the Russian Orthodox Church under Soviet communism, who were prepared to tone down their social teaching, comply with communism, even collaborate with the KGB in the repression of the Church, as long as they were allowed in one or two churches to celebrate the Orthodox liturgy in all its splendour.

Purity

It is difficult for us to imagine the spiritual force of the Jewish purity laws at the time of Jesus. They went back to laws codified in the books of Leviticus and Deuteronomy. They are particularly concerned with food – not only with what foods may or may not be eaten, but with how to prevent impurities creeping in while food was being prepared. Other concerns were to prevent defilement from natural bodily emissions. Semen, menstrual blood, discharges from infections, or skin diseases all made people impure. So did any contact with death or dead bodies, whether human or animal. The purity laws were not primarily to do with hygiene. Nobody (except the obsessive Essenes) bothered much about urine or excrement or thought that they were spiritually dangerous. Pollution was more like invisible spiritual bacteria and was thought to do real harm to people's well-being and relationship with God. Most ancient and modern societies have taboos, behaviours and states of being that are regarded as dangerous or chaotic in some way for everyone. Jews are not the only ones to think that if people or material objects are defiled in some way, a kind of chaos ensues, which must then be set right for normal life to be established.

The Jews had a highly exalted view of God. He was invisible, inaccessible, utterly holy, spiritual, and beyond the material world that he had created. This holiness was God's most beautiful and fascinating attribute, but it was also dangerous to humanity. The holy books of Jewish Scripture came to be described as books that defiled the hands: the handling of them brought people into contact with holiness and that in itself was defiling, almost like radioactivity. The power of unmediated holiness could be destructive, but the purity laws allowed for people to be in contact with God without endangering themselves and others. They were a form of taboo, separating off the things of messy earth – death, sex and disease – from the radiant glory of God's presence, his ineffable and unspeakable name. To be polluted, impure or unclean was to be in a state of sin. This was a danger not only to oneself, but also to others because impurity was thought to be highly contagious. The only way to be safe was by extreme caution and extreme vigilance. Washing, bathing and purifying oneself was a way of life.

How did the priests maintain strict purity? On the southern side of the temple mount archaeologists have discovered a buried grotto, which was once a ritual bath. There were two separate staircases enabling people to walk in and out without mingling with one another; the clean and the unclean must be kept separate. No Jew could enter the temple without first purifying himself. Many ritual baths have been found around the temple, including one that is so big it is thought to have been designed not for people, but for furniture that had been defiled. A bed stained with menstrual blood, for example, would have been dipped in the bath to restore purity.

Ritual baths were part of everyday Jewish life, and Jesus would have taken them. They are a part of many religious traditions today. Muslims wash before worship and at other times, in prescribed ways; Christian priests wash their hands before offering the sacrifice of the mass. But the Jewish purity system went further than ensuring that individuals were ritually clean for the worship of God. In the context of loss of national independence, ritual purity for the nation remained the sole assurance of the Jewish relationship with God. The Jews could not avoid contact with the impure Gentile world, but they could protect themselves from it as far as possible by withdrawing into more and more extreme forms of distinctive purity. By maintaining ritual holiness, the priests believed that they were assured of God's continued favour towards them.

There were some who were excluded from practising their faith no matter how many ritual baths they might take, and at the time of Jesus there were whole classes of people who were defiled in ways that simply couldn't be washed off. They were unclean in their very being, cut off from society and unacceptable to God. Those were the people Jesus reached out to.

He had lived his life in the shadow of the temple. He may have visited Sepphoris and seen the enormous lengths that rich, priestly families would go to in order to maintain purity. He may have had contact with the Essenes, possibly through John the Baptist, and seen how their lives were driven by the desire to be even purer than their fellow Jews. Jesus had received his own vocation in the ritual immersion of baptism; in that dramatic plunge into the water of the Jordan he had sensed that he was set apart for a sacred task. He had withdrawn into the wilderness to work out what was being asked of him.

Now, at about the age of thirty, having been turned out of his home town, Jesus found himself drawn to the poor and the ordinary, and even beyond them, to the sick and excluded who had no place within the Jewish community. Instead of shunning them, which would have been natural enough, Jesus found himself seeing them as people especially targeted by God for the invitation into God's kingdom. They, the outsiders and the unclean, were the very people for whom the kingdom was coming. What could he do for them?

4

INSIDERS AND OUTSIDERS

In the old Muslim quarter of Jerusalem there is a magnificent Crusader church, strong and simply built in the Norman style with its thick and weighty pillars and round stone arches. It has a resonant acoustic: the human voice soars against stone and echoes around the walls for a full ten seconds. Not surprisingly, it is a favourite stopping place for choirs on tour or pilgrimage in Jerusalem who love to hear themselves sing in an acoustic that is forgiving enough to drown minor inaccuracies. This is the Church of St Anne, traditionally the home of the Virgin Mary's parents, Anne and Joachim.

Next to the Norman church archaeologists have discovered the remains of another church. This one is from the fifth century and it is at the site of an ancient pool. It has features that have led to its being identified as Bethesda, where a miracle took place which is recounted in the fifth chapter of John's Gospel. John says that Jesus was in Jerusalem for an unspecified feast of the Jews. He describes a pool, located 'near the Sheep Gate', which was surrounded by five porticoes. When the archaeologists excavated the site they found what could well be the remains of these porticoes buried at the bottom of what was once a pool. It is clear from the remains of the church that these older arches were incorporated into the fifth-century structure to support one side of it. If this is the site described by John it is easy to imagine how the arched colonnade could have given shelter to large numbers of invalids: the blind, the lame, and the paralysed. One man, according to John, had been lying there, perhaps brought out daily by relatives and friends, for thirty-eight years.

The whole scene that John describes is plausible against the background of what we are discovering about Jesus and the purity system. He portrays a crowd of sick people sheltering beside a pool in the shadow of the temple from which they were excluded by reason of their condition. The scene also makes sense of our knowledge of Jerusalem at the time of Jesus. One of the Hasmonean High Priests, Simon, had built two pools at the beginning of the second century BC to help supply the temple. The two pools became unnecessary after Herod the Great had a new and larger pool built closer to the temple, but they continued to fill up with rainwater in the winter. In spite of the construction of Herod's pool, these earlier pools would have maintained their association with purity and healing. In fact, after the destruction of Jerusalem when the Romans were trying to impose their culture on the city, the site became a shrine to the god Asclepius. This god is often shown holding a staff with two serpents intertwined. He is the god of healing and his serpent staff is still a symbol used by pharmacists and on medical crests. Archaeologists have found small votive offerings to the god at the site of the High Priest's pools.

From the account in John's Gospel it appears that the pools had always been regarded as sacred. That was why they attracted such interest from the handicapped; it was their last chance. Jesus asks the sick man the apparently obvious question of whether he wants to be healed. The man makes the pathetic response that he tries to get into the water 'when it is troubled', but by the time he is able to haul himself into position to get down the steps someone else has got in front of him. Some ancient manuscripts of this part of the Gospel add the helpful explanation that the water was 'troubled' at certain times of the year when an angel paid a fleeting visit to the pool. Presumably, the descent of the angel stirred up the water, like a sudden gust of wind. It was believed that whoever managed to get in first after the angelic dip was automatically cured of whatever disease they had.

Jesus, having heard the man's sad story, invited him to take up his pallet, or mattress, and walk, which he did, immediately. John adds that this all happened on the Sabbath. Unfortunately, as the man made his way home he met people who told him that he should not be carrying his pallet, as it was an infringement of Sabbath regulations. They asked him who had healed him, to which he could not respond as he did not know. Later Jesus found the man in the temple. Not surprisingly, his first instinct had been to go to the place of reconciliation with God to offer thanks for his healing. Jesus encouraged him in his new-found health, and warned him against falling into sin, lest anything worse should happen to him. The man then continued to tell his story, naming Jesus as his healer. The fact that the cure had occurred on the Sabbath was not forgotten.

The healing of the sick

The Gospels report many instances in which Jesus healed the sick. Whether he did or did not actually heal, he clearly acquired a reputation as a healer. To understand what that meant we need to look at the Jewish attitude to health and healing. The Jews regarded health very much as a gift of God, and the only real cure for sickness was prayer. There were ancient prophets who had gifts of healing. Elisha healed Naaman the Syrian (2 Kings 5:1–14) and Isaiah made a poultice of figs which cured a life-threatening tumour that afflicted King Hezekiah (2 Kings 20:1–11). Prophets were regarded as specially gifted by God; they were able to mediate his healing powers. Traditionally, the Jews tended to be suspicious of doctors. The story of the woman with a haemorrhage, who had not only bled for twelve years, but had 'endured much under many physicians, and had spent all that she had; and she was no better, but rather grew worse' (Mark 5:26), summarises the popular view of doctors at the time: they take all your money and do not make you well. Admittedly some Jewish writings, especially from those who were well acquainted with the positive aspects of Hellenistic and Roman medicine, paint a more optimistic picture. Sirach tells sensible people not to despise medicine or doctors' skills, for both are created by God (Sirach 38:8). But even he reverts to the more common Jewish view that it is prayer that offers the best hope of healing. Physicians themselves should have recourse to prayer so that God will help them both in their diagnosis and in their efforts to preserve life.

There was a long-running link in Jewish thinking between sickness and sin. Since God is the source of life and well-being, sickness or infirmity must be a sign of divine disapproval, a warning that things are amiss with one's life as a whole. Sick people were always being told to examine their lives and confess their sins. Jesus' warning to the man he had healed not to sin, lest worse befall him, expresses this widely held view. The psalms are full of prayers to God to heal and give relief to individual sufferers. The book of Deuteronomy warns of dreadful diseases that will afflict those who forget God. It is only the book of Job that really challenges the link between sickness and sin. Elsewhere, it is taken for granted.

The social consequences of chronic sickness were dire. Because large numbers of the chronically sick were ritually impure according to the priestly codes, they were not only excluded from religious life, but were also cut off from any kind of social or financial support. All too easily they became homeless beggars. The underlying assumption was that since God had rejected them by making them ill in the first place, everyone else could reject them too. To get close to them was to endanger oneself both physically and spiritually. Without money, few could afford doctors. So there was little left for the ill and the infirm to do other than gather around a place like the healing pool in Jerusalem hoping beyond hope that the angel might descend just for them.

In the Old Testament Scriptures, the healing of individuals and societies was deferred to God's glorious future. When the kingdom came, when the Lord returned to Zion, then 'the eyes of the blind shall be opened, and the ears of the deaf unstopped; then the lame shall leap like a deer, and the tongue of the speechless sing for joy' (Isaiah 35:5–6a). Then, in the hoped-for future, but not now.

No wonder the chronically sick looked for unorthodox healers; it was their only way back into society and into a relationship with God. Jesus was far from being the only first-century figure who had a reputation as a healer. In recent years Jewish scholars have brought to prominence some fascinating parallels between Jesus and other contemporary holy men from Galilee who displayed gifts of healing. Their deeds and life stories are recorded in the *Mishnah* and other Jewish writings.

Hanina ben Dosa

One of the most interesting is an eccentric and engaging character known as Hanina ben (son of) Dosa. The sources about his life imply that he lived in the first century, so he was a near-contemporary of Jesus. His tomb is just north of Nazareth on the outskirts of the town of Araba, and has been a holy place for Jews for the last 2,000 years.

Hanina was regarded as a prophet; like Jesus, he was sometimes compared to Elijah. Hanina was also a man of profound prayer. He would spend a full hour preparing for prayer – an hour in which he would not let anything interrupt his concentration. He had a peculiar sense of intimacy with God which seemed to give him protection from dangers that afflicted other people. He was once bitten by a snake which did him no harm. On the contrary, the story grew up that the snake had died as a result of its biting Hanina! He was known as a healer and the stories about him describe how some of the leading personalities of the day requested his help. On one occasion, the son of a famous Pharisee, Gamaliel, was ill with a fever. Two disciples of Gamaliel were sent on the long journey to Galilee to ask for the holy man's help. When they made their request, Hanina withdrew to an upper room and prayed. He came down again some time later and told them to go home, because the fever had left the boy. This is very reminiscent of some of the healings of Jesus. Both Hanina and Jesus had the power to heal at a distance and both knew when their prayer had been answered. When Hanina was challenged by the visiting disciples about the cure of Gamaliel's son, he explained that he always knew if a prayer for healing had been successful because the prayer had been fluent in his mouth. Jesus, too, was aware of a healing having been successful. When the woman with the twelve-year haemorrhage touched Jesus' clothes and was healed, Jesus asked who had touched him because he had felt the power leave his body. Both saw healing as a spiritual matter. They were both dependent on the source of healing: God himself.

Curiously, Hanina, like Jesus, also attracted criticism. In part this was because people from Judea thought the Galileans a bit rough and unorthodox. The Galileans were known, apart perhaps from the rich in up-market Sepphoris, as less than punctilious in their observance of the law. Hanina was once severely criticised for walking alone through the streets at night, an infringement of the rules of social propriety. But the story turns to his advantage. On the way he met the queen of the devils who said she would have harmed him had she not known who he was. Hanina responded by banishing her from every inhabited place.

Hanina is also reported to have had the power to make rain and stop it again. In this respect he is in the tradition of Elijah, who summoned up a drought in the reign of the wicked king Ahab (1 Kings 17:1).

Stories of figures like Hanina ben Dosa have an entertaining quality. He, and others like him, were regarded by later ages as pious *enfants terribles*. They lived on the margins of convention, attracting admiration and criticism in equal measure. They reflect a tension between urban and country religion, Judea and Galilee, south and north, the priestly and the prophetic. But first-century Judaism could handle such tensions without them leading to people getting arrested and executed. Hanina died in peace and has been revered ever since. Why did Jesus' healings lead to his crucifixion?

The answer must be that Jesus was offering more than a cure. He was in some way positively encouraging large numbers of sick and vulnerable people to take back their full identity as Jews and declare that they were re-joining the community that had declared them impure.

Why this caused a problem needs to be teased out. One reason is that, as in the case of the healing of the paralysed man by the pool, Jesus seems to have had no qualms about healing on the Sabbath. He even quotes precedents for infringing Sabbath laws. We now know from Rabbinic literature that Jesus' attitude was not unusual in this respect. Among the Pharisees, many would have agreed with him that life and health come before the rigid observation of the Sabbath. But in the heightened atmosphere of an excessive interest in purity, a Sabbath cure from a Galilean preacher might have raised eyebrows.

What people would have found more disturbing was Jesus' own attitude to the sick. While the temple was inaccessible to most of the sick and infirm, Jesus was highly accessible to those who needed him. The priests would go to any lengths to avoid physical contact with disease, but Jesus was prepared to touch those people who were both ritually unclean and physically revolting. The touching of a leper (Mark 1:40–4), whose contagious illness was among the most dreaded in Jewish society, marked Jesus out as either extremely reckless or brave beyond common sense. (Not that all those called lepers actually were sufferers of this disease; so great was the fear of leprosy that a range of less severe skin diseases would have been categorised as leprosy, with all the appalling consequences for those who suffered them.) To be touched by an endlessly menstruating woman (Mark 5:27) would have been a horrible, defiling experience for a normal male Jew. The woman, totally aware of this, tried to conceal her action, but Jesus gently sought her out and reassured her. No doubt in some minds he tainted himself by being prepared to touch such people or let them touch him. It was a breach of religious and social etiquette. The physically handicapped were not treated as real human beings; convention required that they were either to be despised or pitied – but Jesus did neither.

If there were, as seems likely, very large numbers of chronically ill and infirm people who were attracted to Jesus it is easy to see why he became a controversial figure. Wherever he went would have been a walk-in clinic. But it is important to notice that not all were healed. Matthew and Mark tell us rather touchingly that on one occasion when he returned to his home town of Nazareth, Jesus could do very little for anyone. A few sick people were cured, but Jesus found his powers were restricted because of the unbelief that met him (Mark 6:5–6; Matthew 13:58). Faith was needed to effect a cure.

At the heart of the difficulties raised by Jesus' healings was the issue of forgiveness. Accepting the link between sickness and sin, Jesus announced to the sick that they were forgiven and told them to go in peace. Jesus knew the rules. Those who had been sick had to 'pass' the criteria laid down by the priests. Perhaps that is why, at the beginning of his career as a preacher and healer, he insists that a leper he has healed goes and shows himself to the priest and offers the prescribed thank-offering 'as a proof to the people' (Mark 1:40–4). This would give him assurance of forgiveness and permit him to rejoin the community. In this case Jesus seems perfectly willing to live within the rules of the purity system.

However, hard on the heels of that account comes the story of the healing of a paralysed man who was let down through the flimsy roof into the house where Jesus was preaching (Mark

2:1–12). On this other occasion Jesus was prepared to bypass the priestly system altogether, declaring forgiveness even before he performed the healing. This was immediately interpreted as blasphemy. No one could forgive but God alone, and the way God forgave was through sacrifice offered at the temple. We begin to see how Jesus' healing of the sick was not simply an act of kindness (though the Gospels stress that he was often deeply moved by the plight of those who cried out for his help); it was also a symbolic act that challenged the purity laws as deeply as it met the healing and restoration they were aiming to achieve. If forgiveness could be given apart from the temple, then what did it say about the power and prestige of the priesthood?

The disturbed and the possessed

Another category of people who were excluded from society were those with illnesses that were thought to be caused by demons. These included some frightening illnesses we now know to have organic causes, such as epilepsy and schizophrenia. A whole range of mental problems, dementias and personality disturbances excluded people from full participation in Jewish life. The strange and the sad, the hysterical, and those whose minds and bodies made them act bizarrely, represented chaos and disorder. In a pre-scientific society such people were thought to be infected with evil, and invading demons were the obvious explanation of their plight. Because of this, many of them not only lost their place in society, but were rejected by their families. They were forced to live outside the boundaries of society, in the wilderness or in caves, like outlaws.

Jesus' reputation as a healer extended to his being seen as an exorcist; he was thought to have direct contact with the spiritual realm. He could speak to the demons and command them to depart. One of his first reported miracles in Mark's Gospel (Mark 1:23 ff) involves him in a dialogue with a demon afflicting a man who has somehow stumbled into the synagogue at Capernaum. The demon cries out, 'What have you to do with us, Jesus of Nazareth? Have you come to destroy us? I know who you are, the Holy One of God!' Hanina ben Dosa also conversed with demons and banished them, but there is something in the urgency of the demon's response to Jesus that suggests that more was going on than a one-off encounter between an evil supernatural presence and a holy man. The demon challenges Jesus as though it has good reason to fear his purpose. The art of the Gospel writers is to make us feel the tangible sense of threat that Jesus posed to the occupying demon. It recognises that Jesus has come to drive it out – and perhaps not only this one demon, but others too.

One remarkable exorcism is recounted in the Gospels of Matthew, Mark and Luke (Matthew 8:28–34; Mark 5:1–20; Luke 8:26–39). It takes place across the lake in a land called variously the land of the Gadarenes, or the Gergesenes, or Gerasenes. A demoniac (though Matthew says there were two) is living in a graveyard. He is so violent and disturbed that his neighbours have tried to restrain him with chains and fetters, but he has broken them all. His cries are terrible, and he injures himself with stones. On seeing Jesus approach he runs to worship him, crying out a challenge to him at the same time. The confusion of the poor man is beautifully described. The Gospels are saying that he sees his salvation as Jesus approaches, but it is also a torment. Jesus asks the demoniac his name, to which he replies, again with the exquisite clarity that sometimes accompanies madness, 'My name is Legion, for we are many.' The demons, recognising that they will not be able to remain in possession of the man for much longer, beg Jesus not to drive them out of the country altogether, but to let them enter a herd of pigs. (It must have been an area populated largely by non-Jews.) Jesus gave permission for the demons to possess the pigs and they did. The force of their invasion drove the pigs over the cliff face and all 2,000 of them rushed over the edge and were drowned in the sea. It is a weird story, and not easy for us to assimilate with our very different views of mental illness. But what is striking about the story is that in spite of the drama of the man's sickness, Jesus seems to be able to talk to him quietly and to reach his tormented spirit. Even though the man has frightened all his neighbours and himself, Jesus is able to restore him to sanity. When people came to see what had happened to the man, they found him talking to Jesus 'clothed and in his right mind' (Mark 5:15). Matthew adds that the local townsfolk were so disturbed by the episode that they begged Jesus to go away and not return.

What is also particularly interesting about this story is that although the Gospel writers seem unsure about where this miracle is reported to have occurred, a site has been recently identified that could well be the original location. Umm Keiss contains the remains of the ancient town of Gadera, which, in the second century, boasted a magnificent complex of Roman baths. Even before that it was noted for its hot, natural pools that were thought to have healing qualities. The town is on the south side of the Sea of Galilee in an area known as the Decapolis. This is the region to the south and east of the Jordan in which there were ten independent cities founded originally by Alexander the Great. At the time of Jesus these remained cosmopolitan communities where temples and synagogues would be found alongside each other. Jew and pagan would trade and mix as far they could under the wider cultural umbrella of whatever colonial power was in the ascendancy.

Recent excavations have uncovered the remains of a fourth-century church, which is so large that it must have been connected to a site of major importance. The church has no less than five aisles, which suggests that it was visited by large numbers of pilgrims. Digging down beneath the foundations, archaeologists have discovered a Roman tomb that has been dated to the year AD 25, just seven years before the traditional date of the crucifixion. The strange thing is that the church has a hole in the floor that looks right down on to the tomb. The tomb itself is in an easily identified spot; it is just under an archway that marks the western city boundary. The Christians who built the church have done nothing to 'christianise' the tomb. They have neither destroyed it, replaced it, nor attempted to mark it with crosses or symbols of resurrection. For some reason, they wanted to preserve it as it was.

It is a serious possibility that this was one of the tombs that provided a home for the Gadarene demoniac. It has been preserved under the church to mark the place of his exorcism.

The exorcism of the Gadarene demoniac was one of seven such exorcisms attributed to Jesus in the Gospels. One that is not described in any detail is the healing of Mary Magdalene, who became one of his closest female disciples. Her name suggests that she came from Magdala, which was an urban centre on the west of the Sea of Galilee, economically important as a salt market. She was apparently healed of seven devils.

Jesus was a man of his age. He clearly believed in demons and spirits, a whole invisible world of supernatural forces, both evil and angelic. His exorcisms would have contained their own religious message to the priestly authorities, and he recognised that there were forces of evil at work in individuals. But he went further than this. He also seems to have implied that his exorcisms were part of a larger campaign that he was waging against a whole network of evil forces. The fact that the devils recognised him and fled was a sign that the grip of these evil forces on individuals and the whole of society was loosening and would soon be broken. In the context of the first century this was a riveting message. Many serious-minded Jews believed that their land was sick in some way: either because it was occupied by foreigners, or because God was distant or, as Josephus suggests, because there was much internal strife within the Jewish community. Many would have wondered whether God would intervene to purge his people and remove the sickness. While the Essenes and the Sadducees and Pharisees argued about the purity law, trying to strengthen their defences against creeping pollution, Jesus' exorcisms, allied to his message of the kingdom, might have made people wonder whether the source of the sickness could possibly be within the religious system itself. Once again, the actions of Jesus pointed accusingly at the temple.

Mark's Gospel reports that as a result of Jesus' fame his own family came to try to restrain him (Mark 3:21 ff). They had heard people say that he was 'beside himself'. This led to speculation that perhaps Jesus himself was possessed by a devil, the pagan 'Lord of the flies' Beelzebul, perhaps (Mark 3:22–7). Jesus replied that it was hardly likely that the devil would want to cast out devils. What would be the point? Why should the chief devil destroy his own troops? If that was indeed what his healings signified, then it was a sign of a fatal conflict within the kingdom of darkness which meant that the reign of Satan was indeed coming to an end, torn apart by internal divisions.

The immoral

Perhaps the most scandalous aspect of Jesus' reputation was that he was known to have reached out to those who were outsiders because they lived immoral lives. Jesus went further than charismatics like Hanina ben Dosa by his willingness simply to spend time in bad company with people who were shunned by decent God-fearing members of society. The Gospels describe him as spending time with prostitutes and tax collectors, people who were probably healthy enough in body and mind, but who were regarded as wicked. On one occasion Jesus was approached by a woman thought to have been a prostitute while he was a dinner guest in the house of a Pharisee. The woman let her tears run on to his feet and then wiped his feet with her hair. She then anointed and massaged his feet with scented oil. It must have been a delicious, sensuous experience for Jesus, and a scandalous perform-ance for the other dinner guests, who were astonished by his apparent naïvety at appearing not to recognise what kind of woman she was. But he was not being naïve. Before he left he told her that her sins were forgiven because 'she has shown great love' (Luke 7:47), implying to his fellow guests that those who had little need of forgiveness might also be lacking in love.

Prostitution was, of course, known in the Jewish world, though not approved of; but the Romans were relaxed about sex and enjoyed sexual jokes and visual pornography. Every town had its brothels, offering a variety of sexual thrills, which were often graphically illustrated on the walls. In the ruined town of Pompeii the way to the brothel was marked by a stone phallus in the road, pointing discreetly in the right direction. In Jewish eyes it would have been easy to see prostitution as a response to Roman demand and Roman immorality.

Tax collectors were a different kind of despised class. The Roman empire was built on taxation, which paid for its roads, armies and cities. Part of the point of conquest was to increase Roman revenues, and the panoply of power required a constant supply of cash. It suited the Romans to delegate the unpleasant task of collecting taxes to local agents, who were allowed a certain freedom in their methods of making people pay up. They also added on their own percentage for the trouble of doing the Romans' dirty work. From the Jewish point of view, tax collectors were quislings: disloyal Jews who exacted money from their fellow-Jews in order to give it to outsiders. Taxation was, for them, a kind of theft.

Tax collectors and prostitutes were offensive not simply because what they did was inherently degrading, but because their way of making a living was dependent on the unclean Gentile world. They were as unclean as the Romans they served. They could only be allowed back into the Jewish community if they earned their forgiveness by following a strict regime of purification as prescribed by the priests.

But Jesus did not end with forgiveness as the reward after a process of penance. Instead, he began with it. The woman who was a sinner was forgiven directly. Her weeping and her evident capacity to show love were sign enough that she was yearning for acceptance. Though some might have seen no evidence of orthodox faith, Jesus said to her that it was indeed her faith that had saved her.

Jesus did not hold the usual view of tax collectors. He might have thought they were lost souls, but his task was to find such and welcome them into the kingdom. One of his funniest and most memorable stories contrasts a Pharisee and a tax collector going to pray before the temple (Luke 18:9–14). The Pharisee begins his prayer by giving thanks to God that he is not like other people and then lists his moral and spiritual achievements. The tax collector does not dare come close to the temple and will not even look up to heaven, but beats his breast and asks God to have mercy upon him. It is the tax collector, Jesus points out, who goes home as a righteous man in God's sight, not the Pharisee.

Luke also tells the enchanting story of the wealthy tax collector Zacchaeus who lived in Jericho (Luke 19:1–9). When Jesus passed through the town, Zacchaeus came out to see him. Because he was shorter than average, Zacchaeus climbed into a sycamore tree to get a good view. (Perhaps also because he hoped to remain concealed.) As Jesus passed by he looked up and called Zacchaeus down with the words, 'I must stay at your house today'. Zacchaeus received Jesus into his house and entertained him, and then declared his intention to give half his wealth to the poor and recompense any whom he had defrauded. For Jesus this was the moment of salvation: when the tax collector rediscovered his Jewish inheritance and began to change his life. Salvation has nothing to do with ritual baths or earning forgiveness by the kind of repentance that can be clinically measured by a priest.

Jesus' apparent willingness to forgive sins directly was his most blatant challenge to the temple and the purity system. From Jesus' point of view he was not transgressing the deep instincts of Judaism. He would have believed that he was fulfilling the very essence of the law that expresses the generosity and compassion of God. The law encouraged repentance and forgiveness. There was no absolute need for sinners to go through hurdles designed by the priestly classes. Instead, Jesus thought that his fellow Jews should fulfil the law by recognising the right all Jews had to return to God, no matter what they had done, or however much they were regarded as outsiders. He also knew that people who are bludgeoned by the exclusion of others and their own sense of unworthiness are unlikely to find change possible. Repentance is a response to the generosity of God. So often Jesus told sinners that they were forgiven before they owned up to any sins or even said they were sorry.

The weeping woman at the dinner party and the little man climbing into the tree both demonstrated by their actions that they were ready to change their lives. By proclaiming forgiveness Jesus was expressing something both old and new: that God comes to meet sinners more than halfway. Forgiveness precedes and encourages repentance. The prodigal son (Luke 15:11–32) is greeted by his father and welcomed home before he gets a chance to make his carefully prepared speech of regret for bad behaviour.

Jesus has sometimes been seen as a politically correct figure with views on society that coincide with modern socialism and an anything-goes indifference to matters of personal morality. He has sometimes been seen as a first-century (long-haired) hippy. It is certainly true that Jesus was regarded as lax by his contemporaries, but then so were other Galilean holy men. He belongs to that charismatic streak of Galilean Judaism that, taking its inspiration from unconventional figures like Elijah, looks to the heart of things, to the spirit of the law rather than the letter. He certainly did not teach that forgiveness could be taken for granted, nor did he cheapen it by suggesting that the immoral people who came to him had not done anything that needed forgiveness. What he was attempting to do was to show his fellow Jews that they must recognise each other, no matter how far they had fallen. When Zacchaeus declares his willingness to part with half his wealth, Jesus responds, 'Today salvation has come to this house, because he too is a son of Abraham' (Luke 19:9).

In a society that had become quite definite over who really counted as a child of Abraham and who was excluded, Jesus' attitude was generous to the point where many found it offensive and irresponsible. Just at the point where serious Jews ought to be tightening up the rules to preserve their own distinctiveness, Jesus was suggesting that they should shut the rule book and start loving one another. But his critique of priestly power went even further. The Jewish law could be summarised in two commandments: loving God and loving one's neighbour. If, as I have suggested, Jesus thought he was recalling people to the fundamental meaning of the Jewish law, then who counts as a neighbour becomes a crucial issue. It was this question that triggered Jesus' most famous story.

The Good Samaritan

This parable (Luke 10:25–37) is often thought to be a story about being kind and caring to people in need. Margaret Thatcher, the former British Prime Minister, when addressing the General Assembly of the Church of Scotland, interpreted it as a story about the virtues of private wealth. Because the Samaritan had been financially prudent and accumulated personal savings, he was able to help out his needy neighbour. But Jesus was not telling people to open savings accounts or invest in the stock market. The point of his story is much sharper. The story is a satirical attack on some contemporary Jewish attitudes and how far they fell short of the way the law required Jews to be neighbours to one another.

The setting of the story fits well into the landscape of first-century Judea. You really do have to go 'down' from Jerusalem to Jericho. It is a winding road spiralling down from the peaks of Zion to the flats of the Jordan valley; the Dead Sea is not far away. The road is rocky and passes through deserted, dry terrain. In Jesus' time, it was bandit country. The man who fell among thieves could have been any unfortunate traveller. Jesus' listeners would have recognised his plight.

The priest and the Levite who pass him by are grouped together as representatives of the temple and the purity system. Levites were subordinate clergy who did many of the minor and routine tasks in the temple. There were probably about 10,000 of them and they would have been drafted in alongside the priests to work in turns, about 400 at a time. The reason they avoided the unfortunate man was the obvious one of not wanting to compromise their ritual purity. They did not even try to check whether or not the man was dead. Luke says he was left 'half-dead'. They simply could not afford to take the risk of contact with a corpse.

What Jesus was demonstrating was that the ritual requirements of the law had come to take precedence over the most basic commandments. Then comes the shock of the story. The person who does stop to help is not a proper Jew at all, but a heretic, a Samaritan. Samaritans were not regarded as 'neighbours' to Jews, nor did they even have the benefit-of-the-doubt status of strangers. They were enemies. The Samaritans were descendants of Jews who had lived in the old northern kingdom which split away after the death of Solomon, and had lost its independent existence in the Assyrian invasion of 722 BC. The Assyrians had forced many of the leading families into exile and had replaced them with other conquered peoples from Syria and Mesopotamia. From the point of view of the southern Judean Jews, the Samaritans were no longer of pure Jewish blood. The Samaritans offered to help with the restoration of the Jerusalem temple after the Babylonian exile, an offer that was turned down. Their pride stung, the Samaritans proceeded to do all they could to disrupt the work. Eventually, enraged by the superior attitudes of the southerners, the Samaritans built their own temple on Mount Gerizim in about 333 BC. One of the Hasmonean rulers, John Hyrcanus, destroyed this temple and tried to force the Jerusalem version of the faith on to the Samaritans. This was the last straw. When the Roman general Pompey gave them a new independence from the south in AD 64, they decided on a strictly separatist policy. If the Jews were never going to accept them, they would go it alone. Indeed, they regarded themselves as the true Jews who had kept the faith pure. They accepted only the first five books of the Hebrew Scriptures as being revealed by God.

The descendants of these doughty, independent, 'heretical' Jews still live in the hills around Samaria. They are now reduced to a small number, but they still preserve aspects of the ancestral faith that other Jews have lost. Passover, for example, is still celebrated with the slaughter of a large number of lambs.

So what was the significance of Jesus' Good Samaritan? The story dramatised the inadequacies of the purity system by showing that a representative of this most hated and suspect sect could fulfil the meaning of the law better than a priest or a Levite. The system was standing in the way of God's commandments, preventing their fulfilment. It is the Samaritan who acts as a true son of Israel, not the temple dignitaries. If Jews are to know who their neighbour is, they could start by recognising their ancient enemies, the Samaritans, as genuine Jews.

The Samaritan woman

Although the Good Samaritan only appears in Luke's Gospel, it isn't the only time the Samaritans are an issue for Jesus. John tells of an encounter between Jesus and a Samaritan woman (John 4:7-26), who is not only an enemy, but has also lived an immoral life with a succession of five husbands (two more than the Jewish law actually allows), and a lover to whom she is not married. Jesus asks her to draw water from a sacred well for him to drink. Because Jews have no dealings with Samaritans the request shocks her, but she complies and gets into a conversation in which Jesus reveals that he knows about her past life and her present circumstances. To her, this is a sign that Jesus is a prophet, a man who 'told me everything I had ever done' (John 4:29). She then challenges Jesus by asserting the validity of the Samaritan temple site that had been rejected by the Jews, 'you say that the place where people must worship is in Jerusalem'. In response, Jesus neither affirms nor denies the pre-eminence of the Jerusalem temple, but he tells the woman that in the near future God will be worshipped neither in Samaria nor in Jerusalem. He seems to be pointing to a kind of universalism where the valid worship of God does not depend on tribal or ethnic considerations, but rather on whether it takes place 'in spirit and in truth'. John has his own agenda in this, as in many of his stories of Jesus' encounters with individuals, but the story does confirm the fact that Jesus was prepared to look beyond the boundaries of orthodox Judaism for authentic faith. John tells us that as a result of this encounter and the woman's subsequent report about Jesus, many Samaritans came to faith.

Jesus' inclusive instincts did not stop with the Samaritans. He was even prepared to consider the Gentiles as ripe for inclusion.

The centurion's servant

Matthew and Luke (Matthew 8:5–13; Luke 7:1–10) tell a rather poignant story of a centurion at Capernaum whose servant fell sick and who called on Jesus for help. John has a version of the same story in which the centurion is called a royal official, which suggests he was one of Herod Antipas' men rather than a Roman soldier. Luke has one of the centurion's messengers, a Jewish elder, commending him to Jesus because 'he loves our nation', which implies that he was a foreigner. Either way, the centurion or official stationed in Capernaum sounds more like a village policeman than an oppressive enemy, and he had clearly benefited the community because he had paid for a synagogue to be built. That is not to say he was accepted; even if he was Herod's man, it would not have made him a welcome presence. The son of Herod the Great was not much loved and, like his father, was thought to lack Jewish credentials as his ancestors were only converts. The story depends for its force on the centurion or official being a Gentile. In Jewish eyes, however much good he had done, he was still an outsider. Clearly, the centurion's servant is very dear to him and his illness has caused him deep distress. In John's version the sick man is not a servant, but a son. The centurion appeals to Jesus for help, but he does not ask Jesus to visit his home. Perhaps, after years in a small, tightly knit community, he has come to accept that he is not welcome in Jewish homes and does not expect that a Jew would cross his threshold willingly. He explains to Jesus that he knows about authority from his years of military service. If Jesus only 'speaks the word' he trusts that his servant will be healed. Jesus is impressed by this attitude of trust and assures him that the servant will be healed. This is an example of Jesus being able to heal at a distance, and to know that the servant is indeed healed by his word. Jesus goes on to commend the faith of the Gentile as being greater than any he has encountered in Judaism.

For his part, Jesus has acted as 'neighbour' to the centurion in healing the servant. Once again, the accepted definition of neighbour is being challenged. Jesus is going beyond even the summary of the law, 'Love your neighbour as yourself', to a new commandment, 'Love your enemies, and pray for those who persecute you' (Matthew 5:44). How did Jesus come to make this transition?

Outside the boundaries

The Gospels report that, though Jesus never took his healing mission to nearby Sepphoris, he did venture beyond the region of Herod's jurisdiction into the coastlands of what was then part of Syria and today would be the Lebanon. This area was ancient Phoenicia, a region with a long tradition of temple worship to deities honoured throughout the Middle East. It was there (Matthew 15:21–8) that he met a local woman whose daughter was suffering from some form of demon possession. At first Jesus refused to have anything to do with her, saying that he had only been sent to the lost sheep of the house of Israel. But her persistence and courage clearly moved him and he was unable *not* to respond to her request. Again, it was her attitude of trusting faith that impressed him; and once more, he was able to heal at a distance: the woman went away to find her daughter had been healed at the very moment Jesus had spoken the word.

Jesus' encounters with non-Jews are reported in the Gospels, but they are also corroborated by Josephus who found them significant enough to write, 'He won over many Jews and many Greeks.'

Crowds and public miracles

There are constant reports of crowds following Jesus. Mark says it was difficult at times for Jesus to stop for a meal break (Mark 3:20), and all the Gospels say that the only way Jesus could get any time to himself was by getting up hours before daybreak to pray. Just as he gained a reputation as a healer and an exorcist, so he came to be seen by some as an all-purpose miracle worker. As we have seen, Hanina ben Dosa had also acquired a reputation for extraordinary miracles. He was supposed to be able to turn vinegar into oil; he was immune to snake bites; and, like the great prophet Elijah, he could turn the rain on and off.

Jesus' miracles are always explained more purposefully than this, as part of his campaign for the kingdom of God. They don't come across in quite as entertaining a way as Hanina's miracles, which belong to the genre of folktales and tall stories. But they are still hard for modern minds to accept. What do we make of the stories that he walked on water, fed a crowd of 5,000 with five loaves and two fishes, and changed water into wine?

The first thing to remember is the Old Testament background to many of these miracles. Jews were brought up on the story of the Exodus, when God miraculously parted the Red Sea to get them out of captivity. The story was re-told every year at Passover. When people heard of Jesus stilling the storm on the Sea of Galilee (Mark 4:35–41), or walking on the water (Mark 6:47–52), the Exodus would have been in their minds. When the rumours starting spreading that he had fed a crowd in the wilderness with a few loaves of bread and a couple of fish (Mark 6:33–44; 8:1–10), people would have remembered how Elisha had fed one hundred people with twenty barley loaves (2 Kings 4:42–4).

It is important to remember that magical events and mysteries were very much part of the story-teller's art. Nature miracles such as those ascribed to Jesus are found in Greek and Roman literature as well as Jewish, and for that matter, in the folk traditions of Persia and India as well. Before the rise of science people were more ready to gasp at miracles, even if they did not always quite believe them. The nature miracles performed by Jesus are described as provoking awe and amazement. This may be a reflection of a genuine response to the force of Jesus' personality; people simply experienced God at work in him. Something about his authority, daring and tenderness left people wanting to praise God. It is enough to say that miracles have their place in the gospel testimony, especially when they have a clear symbolic meaning. If Jesus walked on water, it must mean he was sent by God. In the end the meaning mattered more than whether he really had walked on water.

Many scholars think that most of the miracle stories emerged after Jesus' death, and were rather like the 'I told you so' fulfilments of prophecy. They pointed to what believers already knew about Jesus: that he was the Son of God, the Messiah. We cannot know this for sure. What we can see in the Gospels, though, is a certain restraint in the telling of these tales. The nature miracles are not just extravagant frivolities. Jesus does not play at rain-making, turning the taps of heaven off or on to suit his convenience or to win acclaim from the crowd. It is perhaps most likely that while Jesus was alive his reputation wasn't based on magic and miracles so much as on his shocking determination to reach out to outsiders. Not the well, but the sick; not the righteous, but the sinners. Not only Jews, but Gentiles too.

There are hints in the Gospels that Jesus may have found this final transition – from a mission only for Jews to one that was potentially for everyone – a hard one to make. Matthew in particular is convinced that Jesus originally intended to stay firmly within the Jewish community. He even commanded his followers to 'go nowhere among the Gentiles, and enter no town of the Samaritans, but go rather to the lost sheep of the house of Israel' (Matthew 10:6). But as Jesus' challenging actions began to trouble his contemporaries, so he began to perceive that the attitude of trusting obedience that was at the heart of Judaism was also to be found outside it. Those Gentiles he encountered and helped seemed able to behave as though they were children of Israel, in contrast to the large numbers of his fellow countrymen who had simply 'lost the plot', forgetting the humane essence of the law in an obsession with the purity code.

In political terms it is easy to see how the purity laws had become so important. They had always been distinctive for the Jews, a sign of their special relationship with God. Nothing marks people off so clearly as their eating habits. Jews simply could not eat with Gentiles: the risks of spiritual contamination were too great. Before the time of Jesus, the Maccabean martyrs had died rather than let pork pass their lips. In the book of Daniel a group of exiled Jewish young men – Daniel, Hananiah, Mishael, and Azariah – were offered all-in dining rights at the table of King Nebuchadnezzar (Daniel 1:3–17). They were granted the best food and wine from the best chefs of Babylon. Daniel, not wishing to defile himself, asked if they could be fed vegetables only. The king was worried that this would damage their health, but after ten days the young Jews were 'sleeker and fatter' than those on the royal rations. For the Jews, real health, both physical and spiritual, required separation from non-Jews. And now, at the time of Jesus, they experienced a kind of exile in their own land. God was distant and they were under foreign influence, so how could they remain true to themselves? The answer was by drawing the lines more tightly round themselves, with more rules, more safeguards, more ritual baths.

People who feel their national identity is under threat always try to preserve the things that make them different. British ex-patriots living far from home develop obsessions with afternoon tea, warm beer and Marmite, and may even start going to church. The Jews had been threatened so often, and had faced deliberate attempts to eradicate their distinctiveness. In Jesus' time the Holy Land, so recently an independent kingdom, had become a small backwater in the huge Roman empire. It was inevitable that the Jews should strive to preserve, and even exaggerate, what made them different. The purity laws became more and more central because they were at the very core of Jewish identity. However, these laws were also dividing society, excluding good Jews and making a mockery of God's love for his people. Jesus, while fully accepting the uniqueness of God's relationship with the Jews, believed that the whole system was unsustainable without radical renewal from within. It is in this light that we should see the essential pattern he gave for prayer: the 'Our Father'.

The Lord's Prayer

This was a special prayer that Jesus composed for his followers when they asked him to teach them how to pray. First, Jesus invited the disciples to begin by calling on God as Father. All Jews would have been familiar with the idea of God as a father to his people, but putting it in the pattern prayer gave it a new emphasis. The prayer went on to hallow, or make holy, the name of God. It looked forward to the coming of the kingdom on earth as in heaven. And then it asked God for the two great human needs, material and spiritual: for daily bread and the forgiveness of sins. Forgiveness was not asked without conditions, though. The catch in the prayer, which makes it so challenging to pray, is that it asks God to forgive us to the extent to which we forgive one another. So it is not only a prayer, but a spiritual path, a way of creating and re-creating neighbourliness between people. Jesus included at the heart of the prayer the insight that people cannot call on God and expect to be received by God without also being available to one another. Forgiveness and reconciliation have horizontal dimensions as well as vertical ones.

The Lord's Prayer is basic to Christian prayer. It is the one prayer that is used by all Christians of all traditions, and it is said in all the languages of the world. It is scarcely possible to imagine an act of Christian worship without it. The original prayer would have been taught by Jesus in Aramaic. Although Aramaic is not spoken in Galilee any more, it has continued to be a living language in remote parts of Syria. It is also used in the Syrian Orthodox Church, which has preserved the language for its worship. So it is possible, still, to hear the Lord's Prayer more or less just as Jesus gave it. Although it was given in a particular context to particular people in a particular language, it has always been recognised as a universal prayer that can be used by the whole human family.

Jesus obviously had a deep concern for right relationships between people. Because God is Father he can be approached by anyone, but people's capacity to approach God depends on their willingness to welcome one another, especially those who have offended them. Forgiveness is central to the message of Jesus, and Christianity has more to say about forgiveness than any other world religion – although this doesn't necessarily mean the followers of Jesus have always been good at it.

From our standpoint in the twenty-first century, we can't help wondering whether there was something in Jesus' personal make-up that drove him to attack the purity laws with such vehemence, and to defend the humanity of those who were excluded.

Ever since the development of psychology we have come to believe that the roots of people's deep concerns lie in their childhood experience. People have always known instinctively that there is more to human character than meets the eye. You only have to read a Greek tragedy or a Shakespearean play to know that there has long been a recognition that our behaviour is influenced by hidden and unconscious forces. But it was not until Sigmund Freud developed his theory of the unconscious that it became acceptable to make links between specific childhood influences and adult beliefs and obsessions. It is only in recent times that people have tried to put Jesus under psychological scrutiny, to ask what it was that drove him to think and act in the way that he did.

Donald Capps is Professor of Psychology at Princeton Theological Seminary in New Jersey. He is also a Freudian psychoanalyst who works with individuals to unlock past memories that are causing them problems in the present. To qualify for his profession he went through years of rigorous analysis himself. Looking from a psychoanalytic point of view at Jesus' life and teaching, he has come to believe that because of the way Jesus was brought up, he felt like an outcast.

He thinks that Jesus' boyhood must have been shadowed by the strange circumstances of his birth. Regardless of whether or not he was virgin-born, there are good grounds for thinking that he was not Joseph's natural child. Joseph, Donald Capps believes, would inevitably have found this painful, a blow perhaps to his male pride and a serious challenge to his loyalty to Mary. Capps has an intriguing theory that though Joseph married Mary, he refused to adopt Jesus as his son. Joseph, he believes, was prepared to save Mary from shame and humiliation, but not to give legitimate status and paternal protection to her child. If this is true, it would have left a scar on Jesus. He might well have felt stigmatised and excluded. It might have been the source of his own sense that God was his father in an intimate and personal way. Donald Capps's theory would also explain why Jesus felt driven to seek out outcasts – he was one himself. The theory might also imply that Jesus might have felt that he was never quite good enough, never quite pure. Only after Jesus' baptism, when he had an overwhelming experience of God as his heavenly Father, did the wound begin to heal and he was free to develop his mission to outsiders.

Like all such psychological theories this one cannot be proved, but it is suggestive. Perhaps it explains why Joseph disappears from the story by the time Jesus becomes an adult. Alternatively, of course, Joseph may have died. However, it may go some way towards explaining why both Matthew and Luke trace Jesus' family tree back through Joseph, as though he actually had adopted him. This would then be a genuine cover-up, an attempt to deny something potentially damaging that was known in some of the circles around Jesus. But of course there can be no certainty in this area. Today we are much more interested in psychology than the Gospel writers were. They give us hints, but no more, and we are left guessing.

Teaching the kingdom

Jesus' reputation may have been built on his actions, but there is abundant evidence that he was also a teacher. Josephus describes him as a 'wise man', and he is frequently addressed as 'Rabbi', which means 'my master' or 'my teacher'. Some of Jesus' most memorable teachings come in story form. The stories are intriguing, vivid, sometimes funny, and often surprisingly inconclusive. It is as though Jesus did not always want to impose a conclusion, but to leave the hearer to react and respond to their own reactions. This, of course, is the mark of a good teacher; you let the pupil teach themselves. It was the same, teasing technique that the great Greek philosopher Socrates employed, and it is classic good practice according to modern theories of adult education. Jesus was a master of the punch line that turns the whole issue back to the person listening. So he ends the story of the Good Samaritan with a question to the lawyer whose original question provoked it, 'Which of these three, do you think, was a neighbour to the man who fell into the hands of the robbers?'

(Luke 10:36). To which the lawyer could not even bear to reply 'the Samaritan', but instead said truthfully, but without the hated word, 'the one who showed him mercy'. The lawyer's spontaneous refusal to speak the word 'Samaritan' exposes the flawed assumption behind his seemingly innocent question. Point made. Point reluctantly taken.

Jesus' stories cover a number of themes. He makes fun of hypocrisy, exposing and satirising the attitudes to purity he found so intolerable. He speaks of the lost being found: a lost sheep, a lost coin, a lost son. He speaks of what the commandments of God actually require in terms of people being neighbours to one another. He paints vivid pictures of the kingdom of God, always pointing to the fact that it is actually breaking out. You can see it before your eyes in the healings, in the exorcisms, in eating and drinking with sinners. It is under your nose, yet you have to look for it. You enter free, yet it costs everything. You can only receive it as a gift, and yet it is the most important discovery anyone can ever make.

Whatever was going on in Jesus' own mind, the combination of this teaching with his actions as a healer must have led to speculation about where all this teaching and action was leading. The kingdom of God sounded so attractive and so immediate, and yet where was it? When would it come?

The sermon on the mount

Jesus' most important teaching about the kingdom of God is given in the sermon on the mount in three chapters (5–7) of St Matthew's Gospel. A few miles from Capernaum a cone-shaped hill overlooks the Sea of Galilee. This is the traditional site of Jesus' famous sermon and is known as the Mount of the Beatitudes. Near the top of it is a curious octagonal church, built in 1938. The eight sides represent the eight blessings that come at the beginning of the sermon on the mount, in which Jesus praises those whose life experience or attitudes have brought them into the kingdom of God. It is a quiet, tranquil site, with one of the best views over the lake. But it is unlikely that Jesus delivered the sermon on the mount in one go, here or anywhere else. He possibly did preach here, though. It would be an obvious setting from which to address a crowd.

The teachings of the sermon on the mount seem to be more of a summary of Jesus' teaching rather than an eye-witness report of a particular sermon. This likelihood is confirmed by what we find in Luke's Gospel, where a rather different version of some of the same teachings is reported as taking place on a plain (Luke 6:17–49).

We have no way of knowing exactly what Jesus' teaching methods were when faced with a large crowd. Perhaps he began with some funny stories, based on his sharp observations of people's social and personal relationships? Unjust judges, absentee landlords, debtors and the indebted – then perhaps the crowd joined in? And out of this Jesus wove some simple, elusive repeated maxims, like the Beatitudes, which were easy to remember because they lodged in the mind and tugged away at the heart and the conscience. Matthew simply tries to codify these teachings in a way that would be striking for Jews brought up on the tradition that Moses had received God's law in the form of the Ten Commandments by going up Mount Sinai. Jesus too, he is saying, preaches the new law from a mountain.

The peasant world that Jesus came from and preached to would have been responsive to novelty. Hard though people's lives were, the peasants Jesus preached to lived before factory methods and time-management made people work as though driven by the clock. Sunrise and sunset were the parameters of the working day. It is not hard to imagine how large crowds could easily have formed around a wandering preacher, who would have provided a distraction from the tedium of manual labour (or, for the unemployed, another day of idleness). There would have been some who realised the radical potential of Jesus' teaching and assumed that he was about to start a revolt. But though some of Jesus' followers appear to have been armed, Jesus never bore arms or advocated violence. In fact, Jesus is remembered for the opposite: for advocating a form of resistance to oppression that was non-violent.

Jesus' teaching on non-violence is so well known that it has become part of everyday language. 'Turning the other cheek' or 'going the extra mile' (Matthew 5:39–42) have often been seen as examples of extraordinary Christian forbearance in response to others' assertive behaviour. This interpretation has been useful to bullies and control freaks. Scandalously, throughout Christian history, women, children, servants, the poor and the working classes have been told to 'turn the other cheek' when wronged. Such meek compliance would earn them a place in heaven, they were told, even if they had to put up with hell on earth to get there. For many people it was the television playwright Dennis Potter who first showed that these teachings of Jesus did not have to be interpreted in this way. In his play about Jesus, *Son of Man*, he had a scene in which Jesus was struck across the face. Jesus 'turned the other cheek' by thrusting the other side of his face towards his assailant, defiance in his eyes, but without the slightest attempt to retaliate. The gesture startled the aggressor, displaying back to him the consequence of violence and making him look rather foolish.

Is this what Jesus meant? One of the scholars who has researched this aspect of the teaching of Jesus is Tom Wright, formerly of Oxford University, and now a Canon of Westminster

Abbey in London. Putting the words of Jesus into context, he shows how Jesus introduces these teachings on retaliation by comparing what he is saying with what had been taught in the past. The law of Moses said injustice should be avenged, but in proportion: 'an eye for an eye, a tooth for a tooth' (Deuteronomy 19:21). In its time this was sensible and humane teaching. We all know that the tendency of those who have been assaulted is to do even more damage in retaliation than has been done to them. But Jesus is facing a situation where violence is not between equals. Ultimately the Romans were in charge and expected compliance. This meant that a different strategy was called for. Tom Wright explains that in the first-century world of Jesus a blow given to the right side of the face was given with the back of the hand. It was meant to humiliate as well as hurt. Turning the face was a kind of defiance, since the aggressor would either have to use the left hand to repeat the blow or strike with an open hand. Either way, turning the other cheek was an assertion of equality, a refusal to accept the intended humiliation. The instincts of the dramatist come together with scholarship to suggest a very different understanding of 'turning the other cheek' from the traditional meek and mild one. It is not about those who are dominated accepting their punishment, but the exact opposite. It requires them to assert their dignity.

It is the same with the instruction of Jesus to 'go an extra mile'. Roman army officers on the move could force subject peoples to carry their gear for a mile, an onerous nuisance, usually met with a fair amount of understandable grumbling. This response merely reinforced the relationship between the powerful and the powerless. But, Jesus says, you can get back your dignity by doing things differently. Take charge of the situation, offer to go further. Refuse the status of subject by presenting yourself as a person who has resources of stamina and goodwill. As Tom Wright puts it, reclaim the moral high ground.

Jesus' lasting role in human history would be assured by his virtual invention of the strategy of non-violent resistance. The creative potential of this strategy has been widely recognised in our century outside the Christian Church. It was Mahatma Gandhi who first put it into practice, with stunning effect, in the struggle for Indian independence from the British. The moral challenge of non-violent resistance has been proved again and again. It really is very difficult to dominate people who refuse to accept that they are being dominated, who, by jokiness and lack of fear, force the aggressor to recognise them as human equals. Non-violent resistance is a nightmare to control because it inspires imitation, and the more people do it, the harder it is to repress. It was the way Nelson Mandela learnt to cope with his long imprisonment on Robben Island. Having a quick temper, his instinct was to rage against his captors, but he soon realised that this only gave them an excuse for seeing him as even less of an equal than they already did. His impotent rage actually boosted their sense of power. But behaving as an equal, insisting on simple dignities being respected and protocol observed to the letter, he gradually won the respect of his captors. It also reinforced among his fellow prisoners a sense of their own dignity and inner resources.

Jesus really believed that the kingdom of God was dawning before his eyes. He wanted people to be ready for it, and the teachings that are preserved in the sermon on the mount are ethics for the new age of God's rule. Jesus also believed that the kingdom was breaking out in the healings and exorcisms he performed. He was freeing the people from their oppression, healing the land of its sickness. It is inevitable that Jesus must have come to see himself as the key agent of God in bringing his rule into being. Whenever he healed, or forgave, the domination of evil was beaten back and the boundaries of God's reign were extended. Why, then, did Jesus not simply continue to heal and forgive and instruct his disciples to do the same? He could well have continued into revered old age, and died as a saintly figure of first-century Judaism, with a tomb like Hanina ben Dosa's that the generations would visit.

The reason is that Jesus had a strong sense of urgency. The nearer the kingdom came, the less time there was for the good news to be heard. The corruption of the temple had reached such a pitch that Jesus came to believe that it would self-destruct or be destroyed. The kingdom was good news for the poor and the suffering, but it was also a judgement on those who had perverted Israel's faith by excluding the ones who truly belonged. It was for Jesus, as God's agent, to confront the forces of darkness at the very heart of his people's life. This is why, in his early thirties, Jesus decided to lay down a final challenge to the authorities by marching, without arms or armies, into the Holy City, Jerusalem, and to the temple, the purest place on earth that had become the heart of darkness.

5

THE TEMPLE AND
THE CROSS

Jesus is the only founder of a new religion to have been tried and executed as a criminal. From the historian's point of view, the story of Jesus ends on the cross. Crucifixion is a peculiarly nasty form of execution; it has been practised in many societies. The Assyrians did it, as did the ancient Persians. Alexander the Great used it, and it was taken over by the Romans. It has always been considered a cruel death. It is public, spectacular, painful, slow and humiliating. There is no privacy or dignity. The body fails in full view of anyone who wants to watch.

Crosses today appear in churches, often as rather beautiful objects. Gold and silver crosses are worn on neck chains or even as earrings. These, of course, disguise the brutality of the crucifixion of Jesus that they are supposed to commemorate. But the horror of the cross is still deeply embedded in Christian spirituality and worship. It fascinates and appals people. That is why there are so many re-enactments of the crucifixion in the form of Passion Plays, devotions like the Stations of the Cross, and Good Friday processions through the streets.

The memory of the cross

Christians down the ages have tried to put themselves through some of the pain of the cross in the belief that the closer they got to sharing the suffering of Jesus, the more their prayers would be heard. The early Christian martyrs believed that they were imitating the passion of Christ by enduring their sufferings bravely. Their contemporaries thought that the martyrs would go straight to heaven, and tried to preserve scraps of bone and tissue from their bodies, believing that they were charged with holiness. Christians who became monks and nuns were often encouraged to inflict pain on themselves, perhaps by wearing a hair-shirt that would irritate the skin, or a rough ring of iron that would cause constant pain and might actually draw blood. Some devotional practices go as far as re-enacting the crucifixion; in the town of San Pedro in the Philippines, volunteers undergo the horror of having nails hammered into the soft tissue of their hands and feet. They are not allowed to scream, though some can't help doing so. Even without such physical assaults, a few Christians seem to produce marks of the nails spontaneously in their hands and feet. These strange wounds, called stigmata, bleed and are taken as a sign of spectacular holiness.

Jesus, rebel against Rome?

Crucifixion was a form of execution reserved for rebels, enemies of the state. Roman citizens were usually exempt. If they committed a criminal offence they were beheaded, which at least was a quick death. Only for the most serious crimes of treason could a Roman citizen be crucified, but non-citizens ran a higher risk of ending up on a Roman cross. The very threat of it was a way of keeping subject peoples and slaves in their place.

Josephus describes a number of mass crucifixions in Judea at the time of the Jewish war. He says that it was common for the victim to be flogged beforehand, and to have to carry the horizontal beam of the cross to the place of execution.

The Jews knew about crucifixion independently, for it was a penalty for robbers. There is a verse in Deuteronomy (21:22–3) that says that a person who is executed must be exposed on a tree and buried before nightfall. This implies that the victim has been executed by another method first, but there are certainly examples of Jews crucifying their enemies. Josephus reports that the Hasmonean king Alexander Jannaeus crucified nearly a thousand Pharisees for treason.

Under Roman rule in Judea, the Jewish authorities had no independent power to sentence criminals to death. The fact that Jesus was crucified is evidence that he was regarded, at the very least, as an unruly and undesirable influence. He endangered the smooth running of the Roman system. The Roman authorities were convinced that he posed enough of a threat to their purposes to get rid of him.

What had Jesus done? He had healed and taught. He had gained a reputation as a worker of miracles. He had welcomed on friendly terms those who were outside the boundaries of normal society, in particular the chronically sick, the mentally ill and those who were regarded as sinful or immoral. Not only did he show kindness to these people, but he declared that their sins were forgiven, bypassing the purity system and challenging the unique authority of the temple. But all this had happened, according to Matthew, Mark and Luke, seventy miles away from the centre of power, in the rural backwaters of Galilee. If Jesus had only been content to stay there, he could probably have carried on for years without being thought of as more than a minor local nuisance to the supporters of Herod Antipas. Some of his followers may even have had connections with the royal household. Luke tells us that one of the women who supported him financially and travelled round with him and his twelve disciples was Joanna, the wife of Herod's steward. There is some evidence that Antipas was aware of his presence. Luke says (Luke 13:31–3) that Jesus had friends who were Pharisees who warned him that Antipas was out to get him, to which Jesus replied that he would carry on regardless and finish what he had come to do. What this might involve, Jesus goes on to describe when he adds that 'it is impossible for a prophet to be killed outside Jerusalem'. For Jesus, Herod Antipas was small fry. He was not the real power in the land.

So Jesus probably regarded it as inevitable that he should go to Jerusalem and confront those who ran the temple and regulated the purity system. Sooner or later he had to put his words and actions to the ultimate test. Matthew, Mark and Luke all agree that Jesus only made one major visit to Jerusalem, though they do not exclude the possibility that he might have gone at other times. This is where there is a serious discrepancy between their versions of events and John's. John has Jesus travelling frequently between Galilee and Judea and sets some of his big confront-ations, like the cleansing of the temple, near the beginning of his public life (John 2:13–22). But most scholars think John wants to highlight Jesus' confrontation with the temple, and so shifts it to the beginning as a kind of headline. Matthew, Mark and Luke are probably more accurate in their chronology.

Luke's Gospel says that Jesus 'set his face' to go to Jerusalem

(Luke 9:51). Mark paints a sombre picture of Jesus striding ahead on the road to Jerusalem while his disciples lagged behind, terrified (Mark 10:32). The implication is that he was determined to see his mission through to the end. He chose to go at the most dangerous time of the year, in the days leading up to the feast of the Passover when Jewish nationalist fervour was at its height. This was the most important week in the life of the temple. Thousands of lambs were to be sacrificed. Visitors would be flooding in from cities all over the Roman world, Jews for whom this might be a once-in-a-lifetime chance to visit the holy city and admire the splendours of the temple service. They brought high expectations, earnest faith, and lots of money for the temple treasury.

The temple and God's presence

To a Jew living in Alexandria or Antioch, or even far away in Rome, the temple was still the visible link with the invisible God of Israel. Familiar with shrines and temples to the myriad divinities of the ancient world, they took a pride in the temple's uniqueness. There was something awe-inspiring in its lack of visual imagery, in the profound silence of the temple service, and the austere emptiness of the holy of holies. The temple was the one place on earth that God had established as a place of his presence. He was there, though not of course in physical form. To Jews, any suggestion that God could be represented by a material object was simply obscene. God was there because he had chosen to put his name there. This belief that the name of God could have an earthly location was the way Jews dealt with the inherent tension in their faith, which required them to believe that God was invisible and beyond physicality, and yet remained linked to his people through the land of Israel, through Jerusalem the holy city, and through the temple itself.

The name of God was a sacred name; four letters of the Hebrew alphabet: YHWH. The name could not be spoken aloud, but the letters were inscribed on the metal plate worn on the High Priest's forehead. The invisible presence of the Almighty was most closely associated with the innermost sanctuary, the empty holy of holies, which was only entered once a year, by the High Priest on the day of atonement. In the ancient temple of Solomon, the holy of holies had housed the ark of the covenant, which may have been seen as a kind of empty throne for the invisible God. The ark had disappeared in the destruction of 586 BC, but the space it once had occupied was still regarded as the place of God's presence.

The spiritual link between temple and people, although it may have appeared stronger than ever thanks to the rebuilding programme of Herod the Great, was actually weakening in the time of Jesus. The vulnerability of the temple to desecration by foreigners was obvious to everyone. Even Herod had managed to offend Jewish sensibilities by erecting a golden eagle at the entrance to the sanctuary. But in spite of the centrality of the temple, the fact that so many Jews were now living out-side the Holy Land meant that other ways of worshipping were actually becoming more important. The temple remained an emotional focus, but most Jews gathered for prayer and study in the synagogues they built in the cities of the empire. The more educated studied Greek philosophy, and some could no longer read the Hebrew Scriptures. There was a tendency, which had always been present in the psalms and the prophets, to spiritualise the language of sacrifice and offering. The Holy Land had lost its independence and, in a sense, God was no longer felt to be as close as Jews assumed he must have been to their forebears.

Sheep being sacrificed today at the Passover Festival in Samaria.

Jeremy Bowen reclines at the 'Last Supper' table in the
Biblical Resources Centre, Jerusalem.

A computer reconstruction of temple priests
outside the temple in Jerusalem.

Inside the temple.

Visitors in the temple courtyard.

The courtyard from the temple colonnade.

One of the volunteers is 'crucified' in the Philippines, Good Friday 2000.

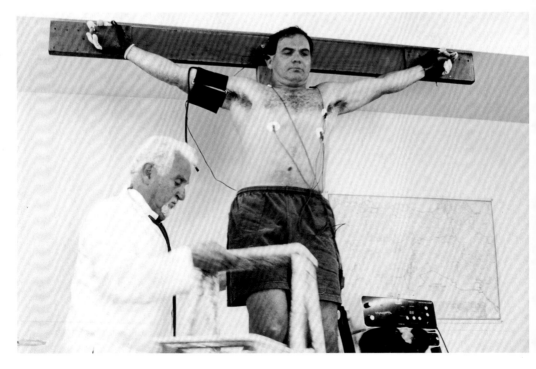

Dr Zugibe carries out a scientific experiment to understand
the process of crucifixion.

A dramatic reconstruction of Jesus being crucified on a tree.

A reconstruction of the women visiting the tomb on Easter morning.

Three first-century Jewish skulls.

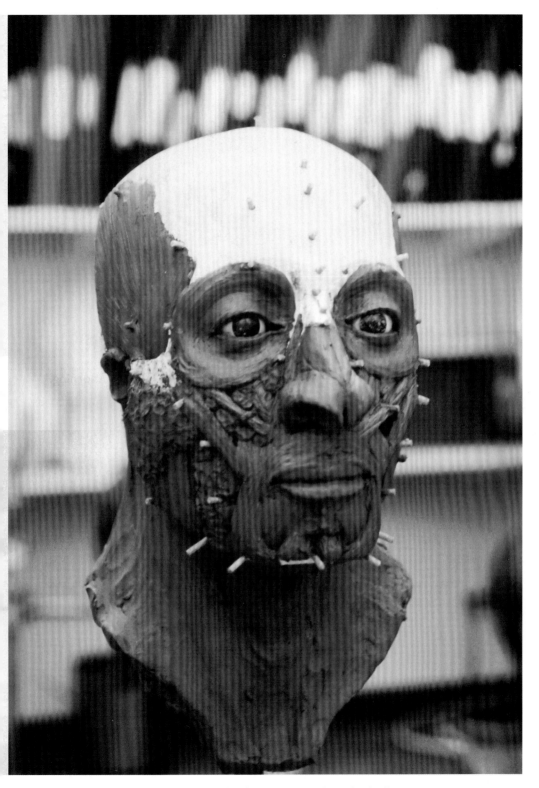

A facial reconstruction of a first-century Jewish skull in process.

A full reconstruction of the face of Jesus based on a first-century skull.

The distance of God

Since the time when the Seleucid kings tried to wipe out the Jewish faith, many Jews had come to feel that God was distant, even absent, from his people. This distance was filled, in part, by a belief in angels and intermediaries of all sorts. All the nations had their special angel. Israel's was Michael, the archangel. But there were lots of other angelic forces between earth and heaven that were thought to have real, if limited, power over the destiny of kingdoms and nations.

The problem of God's absence persisted, though. It was made worse by the fact that as educated Jews became more familiar with Greek philosophy they started to think of God in more abstract terms. Writers like Josephus were familiar with Greek ideas. Their more remote understanding of God contributed to the general loss of certainty about what God was up to.

In contrast to the intellectuals, many fervent Jews simply hoped for a dramatic return of God to save his land and nation. It is this expectation that fuelled the messianic hopes that were so influential at the time of Jesus. There were plenty of prophecies in the Scriptures about the Lord returning to Zion, entering and purifying his temple, and living again among his people. Although these had been written centuries before, and had been partially fulfilled when the temple was restored after the exile, they were never fulfilled with anything like the splendour of the prophets' original vision, leaving plenty of room for new expectations to emerge and fresh hopes to be rekindled.

When Jesus went to Jerusalem, sometime between AD 29 and 33, there were those who would have been well aware of the possibility that God would come to his people, either in person or through a Messiah. If Jesus had been visiting Jerusalem merely as a pilgrim, as Luke says he did as a twelve-year-old boy, he would have entered on foot, possibly in a crowd that would have approached singing the psalms of ascents as they lifted up their eyes to the glories of Mount Zion. As it was, Jesus entered from the Mount of Olives in a way that would provoke the maximum controversy and expectation. The four Gospels, for once, are unanimous in saying that he rode mounted in dramatic fulfilment of a 600-year-old prophecy made at the time of the return from exile: that Jerusalem's king would enter the city in triumph, riding humbly on a donkey.

Jesus enters Jerusalem

If this really happened as the Gospels claim it did, what was Jesus' route? The Gospels say he had made a temporary home at Bethany, a village a little way out of Jerusalem on the Jericho road. From there he had made the arrangements for the disciples to find a tethered donkey at a place called Bethphage, which was near to the Mount of Olives. The details are not clear – which is not surprising considering the momentous weight of interpretation that has been loaded on to the story. We must also remember that the Gospel writers themselves were influenced by the prophecy they were trying to show had been fulfilled, and used details of it to describe the event, because, they reasoned, it must have happened that way.

The traditional entry point, at least since the Middle Ages, was considered to be what is today called the Golden Gate. According to the *Mishnah*, the codification of Jewish law that was completed about 200 years after the time of Jesus, the temple had an eastern gate facing the Mount of Olives.

The Golden Gate today is a blocked-up entrance to the east of the city, which indeed faces the Mount of Olives. It was constructed at the beginning of the Muslim period in the seventh century, but it was probably formed from an earlier entrance that goes back to Herod's original design. One reason given for why the gate was blocked was that it prevented unbelievers getting through to the Muslim holy sites on the temple mount. A legendary version of how the gate came to be blocked tells of the emperor arriving in full imperial regalia to enter the city. As he approached, the stones of the gate fell together to make a solid wall barring his way. When the emperor drew near in a more humble fashion, the gate miraculously unblocked itself.

This gate was not originally associated with Jesus' entry into Jerusalem. It used to be thought that he had come in through the Benjamin gate to the north of the city, but the legends associated with the gate and its location facing the Mount of Olives made it a compelling stage for the drama of Jesus' entry. The Dominican scholar Jerome Murphy-O'Connor (who is the author of the most useful archaeological guidebook for tourists to the Holy Land) says that in the Middle Ages the gate was opened twice a year, on Palm Sunday and on the Feast of the Exaltation of the Cross. After the period of the Crusades, the gate was blocked permanently. Once it had been identified as the gate through which Christ had entered, it was thought fitting that it should remain closed until Christ came again in judgement.

If Jesus did deliberately enter Jerusalem in this way he was inevitably laying down a challenge to the Roman authorities. He was virtually claiming to be the Messiah, the King of the Jews – and not a compliant king like Herod, who was the last before Jesus to claim and be given this title. Jesus was a king who came with the full authority of the mysterious God of the Jews, who had given the whole land of Palestine to his people and claimed their allegiance above that of any earthly ruler. No way could this demonstration be interpreted as innocent.

What was Jesus thinking? Probably the Romans were not the

centre of his concern. They were an obstacle to God's rule, but not the major obstacle. Jesus' demonstration was directed more at the temple itself and those who ran it. It was more focused, more direct and more obviously a response to a real historical crisis than centuries of Christian embroidery has made it.

It has taken years of scholarship and discovery to unravel the detail of Jesus' quarrel with the temple. It used to be thought by scholars a century ago that Jesus was simply a religious genius who had set aside the laws and customs of Judaism altogether in favour of a universalist gospel. Now we know much more about the different sects and parties within Judaism at the time of Jesus, and we can see how he fits into a precise situation in the Jewish world of his time. We know that he had much in common both with the Pharisees and with other charismatic holy men from Galilee. We know that he opposed the temple authorities because of the damaging effect of the purity laws. We know that he offended some of his fellow Jews because he reached out to outsiders. We know that he told his disciples to travel light, to trust God for their daily needs, and not to accumulate possessions. What we have only discovered recently is the scandal of the temple finances.

Temple of greed

During the Six Day War in 1967 Israel gained control of the Jewish quarter of Jerusalem, which had previously been under Jordanian jurisdiction. Archaeologists had a unique opportunity to dig down through layers of hidden history before handing the area over to property developers. It is now covered over with bijou apartments, some of the most prized dwellings in Jerusalem. Meanwhile, the archaeologists were assessing an astonishing discovery. They had found the actual remains of the houses of the priestly aristocracy at the time of Jesus. These were no functional 'tied cottages', they were palaces. For luxury and good taste they could compare with anything in the Roman empire. One particular house became known as the 'Palatial Mansion'. It has a mosaic floor with elaborate, geometric patterns made from tiny cubes of black, red and white stone. The walls were decorated with frescoes that depict fruits and leaves, and skilfully imitate windows or marble pillars or archways. They are clearly Jewish. There are no gods or goddesses, or heroes from ancient myths – even Jewish ones – or any animal decorations. The Jewish owners were as careful about idolatry as they were about purity. The house had bathrooms with effective underfloor heating for the steam baths of the sort that the Romans enjoyed. Mosaic floors in the bathroom guaranteed that they were waterproof. There were also a great number of other baths in the Palatial Mansion, including one with two sets of steps into the bath to avoid any 'cross-contamination' between the clean and the unclean. There is further evidence of the affluent lifestyle enjoyed by the occupants: remains of finely carved wooden furniture; vessels of stone; decorated glass and well-designed pottery; bronze jugs with handles in styles found in other parts of the empire. The priestly owner of this house had the time and resources to be a connoisseur, a Roman gentleman and a Jewish aristocrat all at the same time. Neither wealth nor friendly relations with Rome were a bar to holiness, as long as you remembered to wash off impurity by taking enough ritual baths.

What enabled this lifestyle was an all-powerful gentlemen's agreement between the priests and the Romans. It suited the Romans very well for Judea to be under the authority of the priests. It also suited them to control the appointments system. In exchange, they did what they could to boost the authority of the High Priest's office. They tried to promote popular consent by recruiting from appropriate priestly families, but in the end this was a secondary consideration. What they wanted were compliant men who had good reasons to be grateful for the career boost. Unfortunately, such appointments could never really win the confidence of the people. Everyone knew that the Roman-backed High Priests were chosen to conform. Most of them were fairly spineless characters and they often failed dismally at the job. One such Roman appointee, Joazer ben Boethus, who took over in AD 6, was entrusted to organise a census. It was all so badly handled that it provoked the riot led by Judas the Galilean, which ended up with vast numbers of crucifixions.

The consequence of Roman bungling over the High Priest's office was that the priestly aristocrats tended to be marginalised within the society over which they held authority. It was flattering to be part of the priestly aristocracy, and the financial rewards of running the temple were considerable. But the priests never really had popular support, and this was another reason why Jesus' challenge made him so politically dangerous.

But the priests had one thing in their favour: money. Personal wealth was not a real problem for most Jews, and material possessions are not condemned in the Hebrew Bible. Generally speaking, riches are seen as a sign of God's favour. But there is always an awareness in the Scriptures that riches can lead people astray. The history of Israel began in the poverty of slavery, and the Jews were warned in the Scriptures never to forget their humble origins. Generosity to the poor was required by God. The prophetic books make it clear that when the accumulation of wealth is caused by the exploitation of the poor, God takes the side of the poor. In some of the psalms and proverbs, luxury and extravagance are discouraged even among the rich. The poor are not to be blamed for their poverty, except when it is a result of idleness. It is better to be poor and godly than rich and arrogant.

Some Jews of the first century went even further, and claimed that poverty was morally superior to wealth. Among them were the Qumran community who preserved the Dead Sea scrolls. When Jesus told his disciples that it was hard for the rich to enter the kingdom of God (Mark 10:21–7), he was expressing an attitude that was quite common in Judaism, though not common enough for it not to have baffled the disciples, whose response 'Who then can be saved?' implies that they assumed that the rich had already bought their way to heaven.

What really scandalised Jesus in Jerusalem, as it had in Sepphoris (if he did go there in his boyhood), was the combination of the strictest codes of purity allied to massive wealth. It was as though the Jewish concern for purity was actually being manipulated from the temple deliberately to exclude the poor and the outcast. This could not be what God wanted or desired. It was the heart of the evil that was choking the life of God's people, and doing damage much more fundamental than the Roman presence.

Hosanna to the highest

So Jesus entered Jerusalem, knowing that it was here that he would meet the forces of darkness head on. He seems to have started a spontaneous demonstration in which people waved palm branches and cried 'Hosanna' as they picked up the messianic symbolism. It is interesting that the response to Jesus was not an obvious part of the prophecies he was later seen to have been acting out. No one in the Old Testament writes of palm branches waving as the Messiah entered his city. Perhaps the demonstration all started in good humour, for there must have been something incongruous about a Galilean peasant playing the triumphant Messiah. Significant demonstrations often begin in a light-hearted way with someone poking a bit of fun at those in power. Everyone enjoys themselves until things get out of hand. The student protest in Tiananmen Square in Beijing began in a friendly spirit, until the authorities became threatened and the tanks moved in. Perhaps the crowds around Jesus caught the flavour of satire and cheered a Galilean holy man who could parody the sacred expectations of the Messiah under the very noses of the priests and in the shadow of Herod's temple. No doubt there would have been Roman soldiers, brought in from Caesarea for the festival, perhaps discreetly placed so as not to provoke nationalist fervour, who wondered what on earth was going on.

Yet this first demonstration did not cause an immediate reaction. Perhaps it was all much more low key than it appears in the Gospels. Only in retrospect did it come to have the enormous meaning they give it, so that it was remembered as a fulfilling of prophecy, 'Lo, your king comes to you; triumphant and victorious is he, humble and riding on a donkey, on a colt, the foal of a donkey' (Zechariah 9:9). As John's Gospel puts it: 'His disciples did not understand these things at first; . . . then they remembered that these things had been written of him and had been done to him' (John 12:16).

After the entry into Jerusalem the Gospels differ about what happened next. This may be because Matthew, Mark and Luke have crammed an enormous amount into the last week of Jesus' life and they all have different ways of arranging the material. Some scholars think they have been too artful, and that Jesus must have been in Jerusalem for much longer – perhaps for several months leading up to Passover – for the tensions to build up into the drama of the last days. John, who scatters stories about Jesus in Jerusalem all through his Gospel, may be a good counterbalance to the very tight description offered by the other three, though most scholars still think it probable that Jesus did make only one major visit to the holy city – even if it was rather longer than we might think on the evidence of Matthew, Mark and Luke. Still, they are our best guide, once we realise that they were also writing a kind of Passion Play. They knew the finale they were leading up to and shaped their material into a memorable narrative that has moved people for 2,000 years.

There is considerable evidence that Jesus followed up his initial demonstration with a public announcement to the effect that the temple was about to be destroyed. Mark, Matthew and Luke report Jesus saying this quite frankly and unambiguously. The disciples are full of admiration for the splendid architecture, 'Look, Teacher, what large stones and what large buildings!' (Mark 13:1). To which Jesus replies, 'Do you see these great buildings? Not one stone will be left here upon another; all will be thrown down' (Mark 13:2; Luke 21:5–6; Matthew 24:1–2). The Gospels also report Jesus carrying out another demonstration, this time directed at the financial arrangements from which the temple staff profited.

The cleansing of the temple

Jesus entered the temple with a whip, and then overturned the tables of the money-changers and drove them out, along with the merchants selling birds for sacrifice. These activities took place in the splendid royal portico, at the top of the temple steps, on the temple's south side (Matthew 21:12–13; Mark 11:15–17; Luke 19:45–6). This is the incident that John puts, confusingly, right at the beginning of his Gospel (John 2:13–16), as though to make the point that this was the real issue in Jesus' life, the crucial point of his story. The fact that all four Gospels describe the incident in similar terms means that we can have a high degree of confidence that it actually happened.

Jesus' action was dramatic, and it was clearly an attack on financial corruption. The Gospels suggest that while Jesus had been hanging around the temple precincts he spent some time sitting and watching people bringing gifts to the temple treasury. There must have been a constant stream of visitors, especially in the run-up to Passover. Jesus would have watched them coming from the ritual baths with their offerings. One small incident that made an impression on Jesus was the sight of a poor widow who was only able to put in two copper coins, 'the widow's mite' (Mark 12:41–4; Luke 21:1–4). There are problems about the story, not least in knowing how Jesus was able to see how much the widow put in, and what exactly the 'temple treasury' was. The most likely explanation is that there was some kind of receptacle for free-will offerings. But the meaning of the story is to point to the generosity of the poor woman, who could not afford to pay in the official temple currency, and yet put in what she had. She was one of the outsiders, debarred by her poverty, and yet, as Jesus saw it, infinitely more qualified than the rich to make an offering that God would accept.

To understand why Jesus drove the money-changers out it is important to know how the temple finances worked. The temple retained control of its own currency, and every Jew was obliged to pay the temple tax of half a shekel. The temple authorities decreed that this payment must be made with coins of purest silver, and that meant the silver coins from the coastal city of Tyre. Never mind that they had a pagan symbol on their face, the head of the Tyrian's god Melkart; these were what the temple required. Not only was Tyrian silver required to pay the temple tax, but also all buying and selling within the temple precincts had to be done with the same special coinage. Visitors coming from the baths would have to change their money in order to buy an animal or bird for sacrifice. Even if you were poor and could only afford a pigeon, you still had to have the right coinage. Naturally enough, the money-changers who carried out these transactions expected to get a cut, and the priests expected their share of the profits too. If the poor widow had wanted to make a sacrifice, she too would have had to have enough money to buy silver. We have evidence that Jesus was aware of how the system both robbed, and eventually excluded, the poor. Both Luke and Mark introduce the story of the widow's offering with a preached warning from Jesus – delivered, presumably, within the temple precincts, in which he accuses the scribes of 'devouring' the houses of widows. Their greed ate up the homes of the needy. No wonder there were so many 'outsiders' and that the temple treasury was bursting.

It would be wrong to think that it was only Jesus who objected to financial corruption in the temple. The Pharisees tended not to be aristocrats and were often regarded as champions of the people. They are known to have complained bitterly of priestly excesses. Nor was it only Jesus who realised that the whole temple system was running on borrowed time. A major problem was that the building programme started by Herod would clearly one day be finished; workers who had depended for years on steady wages would be thrown into unemployment. Jesus was not alone in foreseeing the eventual destruction of the temple. According to the Jewish Talmud, the sage Johanan ben Zakkai foretold the destruction of the temple forty years before it happened.

But what was unique about Jesus' demonstration in the temple was that it replayed an incident in Judah's past. Five hundred years earlier the prophet Jeremiah had stood at the entrance of Solomon's temple and preached to those who entered to worship that they should amend their ways (Jeremiah 7:1–7). Jeremiah was all too aware of how the temple was a sign of national and ethnic pride, signifying God's special choice of Jerusalem and Judah. Jeremiah warned people in his sermon: 'Do not trust in these deceptive words: "This is the temple of the LORD, the temple of the LORD, the temple of the LORD." ' He pointed out that the presence of God in the temple was conditional on justice and right dealing. He actually equates the oppression of outsiders, foreigners, orphans and widows with idolatry, and says that God will abandon the temple unless his people live as they are meant to.

Tom Wright points out that by overthrowing the tables of the money-changers Jesus interrupted for a few minutes the whole sacrificial system of the temple. He suspended its sacred power, its cosmic significance. Only God, or a messenger of God, could do that. The expectation that God would revisit his temple was the subject of a prophecy from Malachi: God's messenger will be sent before him to prepare for the Lord to come to his temple. But the Lord comes not to admire or approve, but to judge and cleanse. 'But who can endure the day of his coming, and who can stand when he appears?' (Malachi 3:2). The prophet compares the coming of the Lord of the temple to a refiner's fire, like the fire that is used to purify silver. He says that he will purify the sons of Levi (that is, the sons of priestly families) and refine them until they are capable of presenting right offerings to the Lord. Jesus' cleansing of the temple is a sign of judgement; he is acting as if he were the messenger of the Lord, or even the Lord himself. The arrogance of Jesus is astonishing. He is demonstrating that the monument to purity at the heart of Jewish life is itself impure. The silver coinage that holds the whole system together is filthy and needs to be refined all over again.

But still, according to the Gospels, nothing happened. No one laid a hand on Jesus or tried to prevent his coming or going. The

Gospels suggest that the authorities were afraid that a serious riot would begin if anyone interfered. If this incident occurred weeks or even months before the Passover feast, it is easier to see how Jesus' violent act might have been taken more as a nuisance than a serious threat. For Matthew, Mark and Luke, though, this is the climax of Jesus' mission. He had reached the temple; he had declared its fate. He had acted out God's judgement on it in his sweeping symbolic gesture. Now what?

In the familiar chronology of Matthew, Mark and Luke, the feast of Passover was imminent.

The Last Supper

The most familiar image of the Last Supper, copied and imitated in stained glass and on altars all over the world, is that of Leonardo da Vinci. Jesus looks out from the middle of a long rectangular table surrounded by the twelve disciples. Behind, a suspiciously Italian landscape falls away in perfect perspective. The front of the table comes out to meet us, so that we are not only spectators at the feast, but additional guests. This, of course, is a devotional painting, intended to inspire believers and remind them of holy communion, the Church's commemoration of the Last Supper.

The real Last Supper would have looked very different. The supper took place in a private room, a guest room in Jerusalem. Jesus had been staying at Bethany, not in Jerusalem because it would have been crammed to bursting. With such pressure on accommodation there simply weren't enough rooms available within the city itself.

But Jesus deliberately arranged to eat this meal in Jerusalem. The most obvious reason why is that this was the special meal, known as the *seder*, which Jews down the ages have celebrated on

135

the night of Passover. Matthew, Mark and Luke all agree that the Last Supper was a Passover meal. John's Gospel differs at this point by implying that Jesus ate the Last Supper with his friends before the Passover feast. Sacred law required Jews to eat the Passover within the temple precincts where the sacrificial lambs were being slaughtered. This was obviously impossible with the numbers present in or around Jerusalem, so it was permitted for people to use private houses in the city to eat the Passover lamb. Jesus had made a prior arrangement to borrow a room for the meal. He told the disciples to follow a man carrying a water pot on his head who would lead them to a house (Mark 14:12–15). He gave them a password for the owner of the house who would show them a furnished upper room where they could prepare the meal. There is an intriguing possibility that the man with the water jar may have been an Essene. Usually it was a woman's task to carry water pots in this way, but the Essenes were mostly celibate men and so would have done these tasks themselves.

The meal would have been eaten at a three-sided stone table, and it would have been eaten reclining rather than sitting up. This was in the Roman style. The original Passover meal was eaten standing up like the Hebrew slaves preparing their escape from captivity in Egypt. Normal meals were eaten sitting down, but reclining at Passover was a solemn duty: it symbolised the dignity of the feast with its theme of passing from slavery to freedom. The seating would have had a particular order and formality, one that was not well suited to casual dinnertime conversation. At a three-sided *triclinum*, as the Roman dining arrangement is called, everyone reclines the same way. If you wanted to speak to someone behind you, you had to lean back. This may be the arrangement that is reflected in a verse of John's Gospel where he writes of the disciple Jesus loved reclining close to him (John 13:23). A more traditional translation says that the beloved disciple was 'close to the breast of Jesus'. The *triclinum* arrangement doesn't suggest the posture of manly embrace that the traditional version implies. It could simply be an accurate depiction of normal seating at such an event with Jesus a little way behind John, facing in the same direction. Jesus, as the host, would not have sat in the middle but second from the end. This allowed another person to sit at the end next to him and protect him from possible attack.

It is quite likely that the disciples would have begun the meal in high spirits. After all, Jesus had fulfilled his mission, and the healings and teachings had continued – even in the precincts of the temple itself. No one had tried to stop him. The city itself was full of excitement and the disciples must have felt they were on the crest of a wave that would lead them on to triumph. Perhaps this Passover was the beginning of a new liberation for God's people. Just as God had freed his people in ancient times from the power of the Egyptians, perhaps this very meal spelt the end of Roman rule. Perhaps the kingdom would come in the morning. But as the meal went on Jesus destroyed the upbeat mood by introducing a darker note to the celebration.

The Passover meal began with a kind of *hors d'oeuvre* of bitter herbs. Bread was not introduced until the meal was underway. It was obligatory to drink wine at Passover; four special cups were drunk, all with particular blessings. Three of the four Gospels tell us that Jesus took the bread and a cup of wine as if he were about to pronounce the Passover blessings over them, thanking God for his goodness and mercy. He gave thanks in the normal way but then said of the bread, 'This is my body', and of the wine as he invited them to drink it, 'This is my blood of the new covenant'. Shocking, blasphemous words. Not an announcement of the kingdom's fulfilment, but of a further, ominous delay: 'I will never again drink of the fruit of the vine until that day when I drink it new in the kingdom of God' (Mark 14:25).

Gethsemane

Instead of going directly back to Bethany after the meal, Jesus and three of the disciples crossed the Kidron Valley and stopped on the Mount of Olives in an olive grove called Gethsemane. Olive trees are capable of extraordinarily long life, and the olive trees in Gethsemane are said to be 2,000 years old. It is possible that the very trees standing there today witnessed what happened to Jesus on what turned out to be the last night of his life. Jerome Murphy-O'Connor believes that it was on the way to Gethsemane that the horror of what lay ahead finally hit Jesus. The Kidron Valley was a graveyard at the time. There are plenty of tombs from the first century and earlier that are still visible today. Murphy-O'Connor thinks that Jesus would have caught sight of the tombs in the light of the full moon and this was enough to snap his resolution.

In Gethsemane Jesus was overcome with panic and more or less broke down. The Gospels are quite upfront about this. They do not portray Jesus as heroically calm or confident; he is a wreck. Some ancient Gospel manuscripts actually go as far as to say that in his anguish his sweat fell to the ground like great drops of blood (Luke 22:44). Such a description sounds more poetic than factual, but it does accurately portray a rare phenomenon known to medical science. There are some individuals whose bodies have a response to extreme fear known as *haematidrosis*. What happens to them is that small blood vessels rupture, causing blood to seep into the sweat glands. This makes the person actually sweat blood. The condition has been occasionally observed, not surprisingly, on death row on the eve of executions when prisoners fully realise that they are about to die and that there is no escape.

Although the complete realisation of his imminent death swept over Jesus, all was not yet lost. He could easily have got away. Ten minutes of brisk walking over the Mount of Olives and he could have been on the edge of the desert and safety. Nobody would have found him.

So why did he stay? What we have to reckon with is the probability that Jesus had already foreseen his death, and had come to see it as part of God's plan. Not that he had a suicidal death wish – the one thing the Gethsemane story makes clear is that he was genuinely terrified of death. He had no stoical resignation about dying in a good cause as the philosopher Socrates had when he cheerfully drank the hemlock after being condemned by an Athenian court. Jesus had begun to see that obedience to God required his life to be sacrificed. It was the final outcome of the vocation that began with his baptism, when God adopted him as his beloved son.

It is very likely that Jesus had in his mind the example of other martyrs who had given their lives for the cause of Jewish freedom. Tom Wright points out that we know that the Maccabean martyrs were revered at the time of Jesus. During the oppressive reign of Antiochus Epiphanes the seven Maccabee brothers had been given the choice of eating pork or facing death, and they chose death. They had been horribly tortured. The martyrs claimed that their death was not a defeat, but a victory for God and his rule (2 Maccabees 6). As one brother faced his end he said to the king, 'The Lord God is watching over us.' As another died, he prophesied, 'The king of the universe will raise us up to an everlasting renewal of life, because we have died for his laws.' All showed that they did not believe their deaths were the end, but actually pointed to God's superior power and greatness: their deaths would in some way contribute to the restoration of Israel and the defeat of the Seleucid king. What helped this confidence was a growing belief in the afterlife. This was not prominent in Jewish beliefs until two centuries or so before Christ. Until then, the focus was very much on the continuation of this life. The only immortality people looked forward to was through their children and their children's children, but exposure to other Middle Eastern cultures during and after the exile, coupled with the extreme pressure the Jews suffered under the Seleucids, gave birth to hopes of resurrection and eternal life. The Sadducees, who ran the temple, never accepted belief in the resurrection, but the Pharisees did – and so, probably, did most Jews of Jesus' time. Perhaps it is not surprising that the Sadducees, with nothing else to hope for, clung so tenaciously to the temple and to their own power over it. It would be hard for them to see any point to voluntary death, even in a godly cause. But Jesus could well have come to see his death as the climax of his vocation. He was, after all, playing for the highest possible stakes: the coming of God's kingdom on earth. Perhaps the kingdom could not come until he had given up his life. His life would then be an ultimate sacrifice of himself to God, which God would surely honour by vindicating him.

Just as blind Samson had died as he pulled down the temple of the Philistines, so Jesus had come to accept that he would inevitably perish in the destruction of the temple. Of course, he wished it could have been otherwise. The Gospels say that he prayed to God to 'remove this cup from me'. But in the end he was prepared to go through with the horror of annihilation: 'Not what I want, but what you want' (Mark 14:36).

Judas, traitor or friend?

This interpretation would help to explain a part of the story that has always been difficult to understand: the role of Judas Iscariot. As Jesus finished his prayer in Gethsemane and roused the disciples who had nodded off to sleep, Judas arrived in the garden with an armed gang apparently sent from the priests. He greeted Jesus with a kiss, which was a signal to the heavy mob to seize him. Judas had betrayed Jesus into the hands of his enemies – at least, that is what we always thought. But recent research has gone some way to vindicate Judas.

The scholar William Klassen believes that Judas has been greatly misunderstood. He is mentioned in the Gospels as the last of the twelve. Judas did not come from Galilee, but from Judea – probably from the southern village of Carioth, as implied by his surname. John's Gospel says that Judas acted as treasurer for Jesus and the twelve disciples (John 13:12). This would have been an important role; Jesus and his close disciples needed cash to finance their travels. We know that Jesus received financial support from some of his female followers (Luke 8:3), and that he had in his company women who were higher up the social scale than the male disciples and were wealthy enough to donate funds. Perhaps Joanna, the wife of Herod Antipas' steward, managed to cream off a contribution from the royal treasury! Klassen argues that these funds would have been managed by Judas for the three-year period of Jesus' wandering career. Klassen also thinks that Judas' role among the disciples would have inevitably brought him into contact with the temple. Every time Jesus or the disciples would have come to Jerusalem, there would have been expenses connected with visiting the temple. For example, there was the constant need to pay the temple tax. Judas may even have known people in the temple organisation who became sympathetic to Jesus and his teaching. John's Gospel mentions Nicodemus, 'a ruler of the Jews' and a Pharisee, and all four Gospels mention Joseph of Arimathea as a secret follower. Though theologically unsympathetic to the priests, Nicodemus and Joseph were clearly well placed and influential and would have been well known to the temple authorities.

William Klassen thinks that it was the connections with the temple that made Jesus select Judas for a special task. Jesus needed to make contact directly with the priests – perhaps he still hoped to confront them for the last time with the wickedness of the purity system. Perhaps he still thought he could negotiate with them. Alternatively, he may by now have reckoned that, as God had decreed that he should end up in their hands, it was important that this took place as quickly and efficiently as possible. The problem is that the Bible uses a word for what Judas did that has usually been taken to mean 'betray'. In fact, it also has the more innocent meaning of 'hand over'. Klassen thinks that Judas' role was to manage the handover of Jesus to the priests. There was a transaction fee involved in this arrangement; Judas received money from the priests: thirty pieces of silver. When Jesus saw Judas in the garden it may have been less with dread than relief. He had spent the night wrestling with God's will. Judas' arrival meant the time of wrestling was over. He greeted Judas, calling him 'friend', and returned his kiss.

Though Judas has been vilified for his action, he may have acted not only with the best of intentions, but on Jesus' instructions. Going back to the Last Supper, Jesus said at one point to all the twelve, 'One of you will *hand me over*'. (Remember that the word is usually translated *betray*.) All the disciples at that point ask if they are eligible for this role, and ask, 'Lord, is it I?' (Mark 14:19). But Jesus' enigmatic response indicates Judas, who leaves the table to go about his task. Though this is a possible interpretation of what might lie behind the Gospel text, it is rather a strained one. The disciples are said to have been distressed by Jesus' question, and Jesus himself prophesied that his betrayer would meet a terrible end. But Klassen might respond that these details reflect the dire view of Judas that prevailed in the Church's memory, not what actually happened. He thinks that what Judas was not expecting was the terrible outcome that followed his actions. He was genuinely mortified by the trial and death of Jesus, and it was this that drove him to his ignominious suicide (Matthew 27:5). Since then, he has received short shrift from both the Gospel writers and from history, and been portrayed as dishonest, greedy and treacherous.

The handing over of Jesus was the beginning of the end. At this point the accounts in the Gospels are so overladen with apologetic motives that it is almost impossible to disentangle fact from fiction. Who was to blame for the death of Jesus, the Jews or the Romans? The Gospels try hard to put all the blame on the Jews and to exonerate the Romans altogether – so much so, in fact, that they give the Roman governor, Pontius Pilate, the only good write-up in his life. They try to show him as a just man who wanted to act fairly, but was too weak to cope with the anger of the priests and so reluctantly condemned Jesus to death. So effective has the Gospel writers' whitewash of Pilate been that the Ethiopian Church regards him as a saint. However, both the Jewish historian Josephus and the Roman writer Tacitus paint a different picture. They suggest he was a thoroughly bad lot: cruel and violent, and so unjust that he eventually had to be removed from office and sent home to face trial, after which he was condemned to exile.

The trial of Jesus

The Gospels say that the armed mob who took Jesus from the Garden of Gethsemane brought him first to Caiaphas, the High Priest. Caiaphas interrogated him for some time and then, after debate with the other priests, sent him on to Pilate. Some scholars think that Caiaphas was attempting to try Jesus according to the procedures of the law (Deuteronomy 17:6–7). The questioning was to try to establish evidence for his guilt, which had to be from the testimony of more than one witness. Others argue that the encounter with Caiaphas was made up by the Gospel writers as part of their campaign to discredit the Jewish authorities. Caiaphas, they believe, would have had no authority to act in the way he is portrayed as acting in the Gospels.

Those who dismiss the encounter with Caiaphas argue that Jesus' movement posed a real threat to the Romans, who might well have believed that he was intending some kind of revolutionary action. Luke endorses this as the essence of the complaint against Jesus. In his account, when Jesus is brought to Pilate his accusers say that he has been perverting the nation and forbidding his compatriots to pay taxes to Caesar (Luke 23:2). They also say that he has claimed to be king in a direct challenge to Caesar and has stirred up a spirit of revolt in Galilee and Judea, and even Jerusalem itself. Luke goes on to report that Pilate, having found out that Jesus was a Galilean, sent him for further interrogation to Herod Antipas who happened to be in Jerusalem at the time.

So what support is there for Luke's version? The Gospels report that Jesus had earlier been pressed into a discussion about whether Jews should pay taxes to the emperor (Matthew 22:15 ff; Mark 12:13 ff; Luke 20:20–6). When asked, his answer was, at best, ambiguous: 'Give therefore to the emperor the things that are the emperor's, and to God the things that are God's.' A clever answer, and as evasive as a modern politician's to a tenacious reporter, because it could be taken in two ways. He could have meant that there was no contradiction between the claims of the emperor and the claims of God. People have religious and civic duties and should fulfil both with equal care. (That is how the answer has usually been given by Christian interpreters through the ages.) But in the context of Jewish resentment about the Romans, it could equally well mean, 'Don't pay your taxes because God is your true king, and you owe a foreign emperor nothing!' That certainly would be consistent with Jesus' casual attitude to the temple tax. So there may be some substance to the view that Jesus encouraged people not to pay their taxes. But even if he did question the legitimacy of Roman taxes, this does not mean that his real conflict was with Rome.

In fact, Luke seems to have emphasised the anti-Roman charges because he thought they could be most easily refuted. His account is significantly different from that of Matthew and Mark. For them, what is decisive for Jesus' fate is the interrogation with Caiaphas, the High Priest. Here the real issue is Jesus' threat to destroy the temple. Although attempts are made to lay other charges against Jesus, they are dismissed as false. This is the one change that sticks, and he is guilty, in Caiaphas' eyes, of blasphemy. John's version has Jesus brought to Caiaphas' house and interrogated by Annas, Caiaphas' father-in-law. John does not describe the confrontation with Caiaphas, but says that after it Jesus was delivered to Pilate, who asked him if he were the king of the Jews. Jesus replies that his kingdom is 'not from this world' (John 18:36).

The Gospel writers wanted to play down Rome's involvement in the crucifixion, and they do this in different ways. You can see why all four told their story with mild pro-Roman spin. The early Christians struggled for survival in the Roman empire, and the fact that Jesus had been sentenced to death by a Roman governor was not helpful to their cause. The more they could cast blame on the Jews the better. Over the years this strategy has had appalling consequences. Christians took the Gospel accounts as justifying hatred of the Jews, who as a race were blamed for Christ's death. Matthew describes a Jewish mob baying for Christ's death and saying, 'His blood be on us and on our children' (Matthew 27:25), a verse that seemed to some anti-Semites to justify Christian prejudice against Jews for all generations. It is not surprising that recent scholars have dismissed those elements in the story that suggest there was a huge public clamour for the death of Jesus.

Who killed Jesus?

In fact, both the aristocratic priestly Jews and the Romans had good reasons for getting rid of Jesus. Jesus' main quarrel was with the leaders of his own people. It is not anti-Semitic to take this as a fact; Jesus was a loyal Jew. He did not intend to destroy his people, but to bring them back to God. If this is true, then it is quite plausible that there was some kind of meeting between Jesus and Caiaphas, though this is unlikely to have been a formal trial. If William Klassen's views on the role of Judas are right, Jesus would have wanted this encounter. It was his last chance to challenge the authority of the priests.

And Caiaphas would have wanted to see Jesus, for he needed to find out how strong his movement was and what lay behind it. We understand much better now how fragile the priests' grip on power was in first-century Judea. Their rule had been shored up by Roman authority, but they never had the support of the majority of the people. The cause of reform was popular. Many Pharisees were critical of the temple system; everyone knew about the corruption. The High Priest realised that if Jesus became too successful, his own authority would be threatened and the Romans would withdraw their support from him. It is not necessary to paint Caiaphas and his colleagues as total villains to make sense of this. Caiaphas really believed that the fate of the nation depended on the temple, and the fate of the temple depended on his ability to keep the Romans sweet. He had to find a charge against Jesus that was big enough to convince the Romans that Jesus was a real threat. This may be why Caiaphas did not rest with the accusation that Jesus had prophesied against the temple. This was too obscure for the Roman governor, who would not easily be able to intervene on purely religious matters. Caiaphas went on to accuse Jesus of claiming to be the Messiah. This was an accusation that could bring the Romans in, for messianic claims from Jewish freedom fighters had led to severe reprisals before. The problem was that Messiahs were always popular. If Jesus was condemned as a messianic claimant, it could still spark off a riot and so bring disaster.

But it seems that Jesus himself raised the stakes and played into the hands of his interrogator. He said something that indicated that whatever happened to him now, he would return in judgement on the clouds of heaven and be exalted to the right hand of God. In this statement to Caiaphas, Jesus begins to sound like one of the Maccabean martyrs facing his oppressor in the bold confidence that God would vindicate him. But he does not merely point to God's judgement. He personally associates himself with it, suggesting that he, Jesus, will be the one who returns as judge of those who have judged him: 'From now on you will see the Son of Man seated at the right hand of Power and coming on the clouds of heaven' (Matthew 26:64; Mark 14:62; Luke 22:69-71, and also 21:27-8). Jesus is calling on a prophecy that went back to the year 164 BC, after the death of the

Maccabean martyrs and before the successful conclusion of the Maccabean revolt. This prophecy comes from the book of Daniel. It comes at the end of a sweeping survey of history from a Jewish point of view, depicting the rise and fall of the great empires that had affected God's people over the centuries. At the end of these years of turbulence swirling around the Jewish world, 'one like a Son of Man' would come on the clouds of heaven and be presented to God (Daniel 7:13-14). He would inherit power over all the peoples and nations of the earth. Who is the Son of Man? The clue to his identity comes a few verses later, when, after years in which the Jews have been dominated by the four great kingdoms, God will give the kingdom to 'the saints of the Most High' (Daniel 7:18 and 22). The Son of Man in Daniel is a personification of God's holy people. He is the true Israel, the Jews as God intended them to be. Jesus, then, in claiming to be the Son of Man, is saying that he personally *is* God's holy people. The vocation of Israel is carried by himself. He is both Son of Man and Son of God, the true Israel. In killing him, the priests are setting themselves at war with God's purpose, but when he is vindicated they will see God's purpose fulfilled. Whatever Jesus meant by this it was enough for Caiaphas. This was blasphemy, but it had enough of a threatening political edge to it to make a case to Pilate.

Pilate, too, had plenty to lose from Jesus' growing notoriety. His authority depended on maintaining the peace and making sure that the tax revenues came in. He would have been more than willing to get rid of Jesus if he could be persuaded that he was a genuine threat, either because he had criticised the tax system, or because he threatened the peace of the temple. It is very unlikely that he agonised about what to do with Jesus, as the Gospels suggest (Matthew 27:15-26). Nor did he need a blood-thirsty mob to help him make his decision. These details are almost certainly Gospel embroidery. We can be reasonably confident that Pilate passed the death sentence on Jesus without the least scruple. It was probably one of the easiest decisions of his wretched and undistinguished career.

6

ENDINGS AND
BEGINNINGS

Jesus must have approached the last hours of his life resigned to the idea that the coming of God's kingdom depended on his death. In a way his whole life had prepared him for this. He had weakened in the Garden of Gethsemane, but who wouldn't have? He had been overwhelmed by an immense burden of fear. He had prayed for an escape route as anyone would have done, but none had been given. From a secular, historical and judicial point of view, Jesus' death was the responsibility of both Caiaphas and Pilate, the Jewish leader and the Roman governor. But Jesus had a hand in it too. He could have got away, but finally he chose not to. He even contributed to the serious charges brought against him by claiming to be the Son of Man.

The Holy Sepulchre

The traditional site of both the crucifixion and the tomb of Jesus is a dark, cramped untidy church in Jerusalem, the church of the Holy Sepulchre. From the outside you wouldn't know it was an important monument. In fact, it is almost impossible to tell where it begins and ends, so closely huddled are the surrounding buildings. The outer shell of the church comes from medieval times, but the inner foundations and some of the inner walls go back to the fourth century, to the reign of Constantine, the first Christian emperor. The tradition that this is the authentic site of the crucifixion goes back even earlier. Jerome Murphy-O'Connor claims that there is evidence that the early Christians in Jerusalem prayed in this place until the Jewish War that began in AD 66. Its special status is also attested by the fact that the emperor Hadrian turned it into a pagan temple in AD 135. Hadrian was not fond of Christians or Jews, having just put down the last great Jewish revolt, and he did all he could to eradicate places of worship that could be focuses of dissent. Constantine's builders dug down until they found what they were looking for, 'the venerable and most holy memorial of the Saviour's resurrection' as one early church historian, Eusebius, the Bishop of Caesarea, grandly put it.

The church of the Holy Sepulchre is often a disappointment to tourists, who naturally enough expect the site to be beautiful and inspiring. Not only is the interior dingy, it is pervaded by an air of general chaos, due to the fact that it is run by the authorities of six separate churches. Roman Catholics, Greek Orthodox, Ethiopians, Syrians, Armenians and Copts all occupy bits of it and jealously guard their rights. As they work to different calendars and timetables there is always something going on. Wherever you look there'll be someone wailing or chanting, lighting candles, ringing bells or swinging incense. Processions from one part of the church sweep through with a total disregard for what may be going on in another. It's a nightmare for those who like their worship straight and simple. At times, inter-church relations break down and the chaos descends into mayhem, which has even on occasions included one group throwing stones at another. In recent years the different communities have come to realise that such unchristian behaviour does not go down well with the pious visitors, and they have taken steps to be more diplomatic. But the tensions of the place are ancient and deeply held. When they originally surfaced there was a dispute over who should own the church keys. Naturally enough, each of the competing communities wanted to be in charge. Unable to solve the problem among themselves, it was decided to entrust the keys to two Muslim families. Their descendants still hold them to this day.

Visitors to the site of the crucifixion have to make their way up a narrow staircase to two chapels, one Latin, one Greek. The floor of the chapels rests on a spur of rock. In the Greek orthodox chapel it is possible to reach through a hole beneath the altar to touch the rock beneath. There's something very powerful about stretching out and feeling the ground of the most celebrated execution in human history. So how strong is the evidence that Jesus was crucified on precisely this spot? There's one immediate problem. John's Gospel says definitively that Jesus died outside the walls of the city, yet the Holy Sepulchre is clearly sited within the walls. Fortunately, this problem is easily solved. The area where the church now stands was brought within the city walls when they were extended a decade after the crucifixion.

Around AD 30 this area was a disused quarry, but it had already been used as a burial site. Tombs going back to the first century BC have been found cut into the quarry surface. The Gospels say that Jesus was crucified in a place called Golgotha, which means the place of a skull – a possible reference to the bone-like mound of half-cut rock that must have been left when the quarry was abandoned.

An alternative Calvary

The bustle of the church of the Holy Sepulchre makes it difficult to imagine the rock you can feel beneath your fingers as a relic of the wasteland on which the crucifixion occurred. It is not surprising that some Christians prefer to accept an alternative site for the crucifixion, which was discovered by General Charles Gordon of Khartoum. He was struck by a small hill to the north of the city that he thought looked a bit like a skull. He then worked out an elaborate map of a whole human skeleton, starting from the place of the skull. With a bit of artful juggling he found the pelvis of the skeleton rested on the temple mount, so he assumed that he was right in thinking that his hill was the site where Jesus must have been crucified. Today there is a quiet garden commemorating his discovery, with a conveniently placed first-century tomb opened for people to step into. The 'Garden Tomb' is just like a picture from a child's Bible. The tomb is a cave carved out of the rock; the stone is a discreet round slab which fits neatly over the entrance. It is a good place for quiet reflection and a magnet for tourists, though its peace is somewhat disturbed these days by being next to the local bus station.

However, few take General Gordon's claim seriously. One problem is that it is too far from what would have been the ancient city. There would have been no point in making Jesus drag himself so far away when all that was needed was a reasonably accessible execution ground. Gordon's site also depends on a weird, mystical understanding of the layout of the city and how this might relate to the Bible. Where Gordon got his skeleton map from is not clear, but it has no obvious value as evidence. Nor, it has to be said, does the hill look very like a skull to the unbiased observer.

So the Holy Sepulchre, for all its craziness, remains the most likely site for the crucifixion.

What is a crucifixion?

We all have a picture in our heads of the crucifixion. What we see in our minds is a smoothly planed tall cross with Jesus hanging by the hands from its cross beam. Artists have worked on the image to give it maximum symmetry, so that the body appears to be supported by the straight arms of wood. It is a strangely restful, almost comforting portrayal, in spite of the blood and the nails. In recent years historians have scrutinised contemporary accounts to try to discover a more accurate picture. After all, the cross was an instrument of death. It would be surprising if it were pretty.

In the Biblical Museum of Jerusalem attempts have been made to re-create Roman crosses, following the descriptions given by Josephus. He tells us that it was quite common to execute criminals by the side of roads, using the growing olive trees as the uprights. All that needed to be added was a cross beam, which would be fixed to the tree to allow the execution to take place. Could there have been rooted olive trees in the quarry outside the city wall? Perhaps a tree was specially cut down and positioned there. The Gospels speak of Jesus being compelled to carry his cross, and how, when he failed, a stranger was drafted in. He may have been expected to carry the cross beam to an already standing upright. That, at least, was what normally happened.

The victim was attached to the cross by means of nails. Archaeologists have been eager to find the remains of a crucified victim to check how it was done. Unfortunately, so far the bones of only one such victim have been found. The heel bone of this executed criminal shows a six-and-a-half-inch nail driven through it, suggesting that nails fixed the victim's feet to either side of the upright, an incredibly uncomfortable position, straining at the legs and pelvis. Some experts think that this was an exceptional arrangement, and that more normally the feet were fixed with a single nail through both feet, which were placed one on top of the other. Perhaps different executioners preferred different techniques.

Some experts think that the nails could not have been driven through the hands as the weight of the body would have torn the flesh apart and the victim would have fallen off. The crucified victim found by the archaeologists had scratches on his wrist bones, which may suggest he was nailed through the wrists. Another suggestion is that the victims may have been additionally tied to the cross, which would have helped support the weight of the body. The tradition that Jesus was nailed by the hands is given force by the story in John's Gospel of the disciple Thomas touching the holes in Christ's hands and feet (John 20:27).

Could the nailed hands support the weight of a body? There is only one way to find out and a grisly, if painless, experiment was carried out by Dr Frederick Zugibe from Rockland County, New York. He persuaded student volunteers to mock up a crucifixion and discovered that it was actually possible for a man of average weight to be suspended from the hands. So the traditional picture does match what could well have happened.

The end of the end

The death of Jesus would have been witnessed by his family and close followers. The Gospels all suggest that the male disciples had abandoned him and disappeared, an easy enough thing to do in the crush of Passover. But his mother Mary, Mary Magdalene and several other women stayed beside him to the end. There is no attempt in the Gospels to cover up the brutality of the execution. It was carried out and overseen by Roman guards. It is impossible to know whether Jesus' certainty that his death was necessary for the coming of the kingdom sustained him on the cross, or whether his courage failed again, as it had in Gethsemane. Mark (15:34) and Matthew (27:46) report that as death came near Jesus said the opening words of the twenty-second psalm in Hebrew: 'My God, my God, why have you forsaken me?' This may suggest that Jesus lost his faith that God would vindicate him and died in mental as well as physical torment. On the other hand, the psalm itself ends in triumph, which may indicate that he died with a sense of peace as Luke and John suggest. Luke gives Jesus' last words as a quote from Psalm 36: 'Father, into your hands I commend my spirit' (Luke 23:46), and John has him saying simply, 'It is finished' (John 19:30) as he breathed his last.

Jesus died a loyal Jew, reciting Scripture. Perhaps the familiar words of the psalms brought him comfort. Perhaps he was consciously offering his death as a sacrifice, and recited the psalms as they might be recited to accompany the sacrifices offered in the temple. One thing is clear: Jesus had twice acted out Old Testament prophecies during the build-up to his arrest. The first was in the way he entered Jerusalem. The second was in his cleansing of the temple. Could the manner of his death also have been seen as a fulfilment of prophecy? Does the Old

Testament ever hint that the Messiah might be a suffering Messiah? On the face of it, it seems unlikely. The figure of the Messiah is nearly always a royal person, a leader or king who brings in God's reign through victory. But there is a strand of Old Testament prophecy that may have played itself over in Jesus' mind and helped him to see his death not only in terms of martyrdom, but as a direct fulfilment of God's will, foretold and foreshadowed in the writings of the Hebrew prophets.

The suffering servant

During the exile of the leading families of Judah in Babylonia in the sixth century BC there was a prophet who spoke of a servant of the Lord whose destiny was suffering. There are four prophecies, known as the 'servant songs', in the book of Isaiah, between chapters 40 and 55.

Scholars believe they could not have been composed by the same person who wrote the beginning of the book of Isaiah or the end of it. For this reason, the prophet of the exile is usually called Second Isaiah. Second Isaiah worked among the exiles to convince them that in spite of the awful things that had happened to them, God really was in charge of history. He foresaw the liberation of his people and a glorious return to Jerusalem. The key to this happening was the work of a mysterious individual, a 'servant of the Lord', who was destined to suffer for the sake of his people. This figure would be anointed by the Spirit of God and would bring justice to the nations. He would not achieve this by public rhetoric, but by supporting the weak and vulnerable. His work would not be to judge, but to encourage and heal (Isaiah 41:1–9).

A second prophecy about the servant of the Lord described how he received his vocation from before his birth. He was called to be a preacher. His mouth was 'like a sharp sword'. He would spend his life nurtured and protected by God. In fulfilling his call he would undergo frustration and disappointment. He would discover in the end that his vocation was not only to bring Israel back to the Lord, but to be a light to all the nations (Isaiah 49:1–6).

The third servant song describes how the servant is trained to be a listener. The Lord requires him to listen every morning, not only to the voice of God, but to those he is reaching out to. Unless he can hear as they hear, he cannot bring them the teaching they need. His teaching brings him into conflict with his hearers and he submits himself to physical abuse: 'I gave my back to those who struck me, and my cheeks to those who pulled out the beard; I did not hide my face from insult and spitting' (Isaiah 50:6). This prophecy is curiously similar to the tortures Jesus is put through before the crucifixion, when he is beaten up in the High Priest's house. 'Then they spat in his face and struck him; and some slapped him, saying, "Prophesy to us, you Messiah! Who is it that struck you?" ' (Matthew 26:67–8). Or, in Luke's version, 'Now the men who were holding Jesus began to mock him and beat him; they also blindfolded him and kept asking him, "Prophesy! Who is it that struck you?" They kept heaping many other insults on him' (Luke 22:63–5). In the third song the servant 'sets his face like flint', confident that the Lord God will help him.

The last of the songs is the most important of the four (Isaiah 52:15–53:12). Here the servant is described as prospering in his mission, 'He will be exalted and lifted up, and shall be very high.' But then comes the surprise, 'Just as there were many who were astonished at him – so marred was his appearance, beyond human semblance, and his form beyond that of mortals.' The servant's appearance is horrific. He is lifted up, like a king in glory, but when he is raised all can see that he has been injured. The revelation of God's work through the servant is unbelievable. He has grown up like a shoot in dry ground. He has no natural beauty or attractiveness. He is despised and rejected, written off by his contemporaries. Yet, 'Surely he has borne our infirmities and carried our diseases' (Isaiah 53:4). The prophet says that the servant's suffering is not a waste; it will turn out to be redemptive. His wounds and injuries will bring healing to his people. He is led to the slaughter like a sacrificial lamb, and he is silent in the face of his accusers. But what happens to the servant is the Lord's will; his vocation is to suffer on behalf of his people: 'He bore the sin of many.' After his death he shall see the fruit of his suffering and, at last, *know* that his struggle has not been in vain.

There is nothing quite like these four servant songs in the whole of the Old Testament. It is not clear who Second Isaiah meant by the servant. He was writing for his time and he did not have any special revelation to tell him he was really referring to a crucified Galilean prophet 500 years in the future. He may have been talking about himself, and the struggles of his own vocation. He may have been referring to the vocation of Israel as a whole, or the exiled remnant of Israel. We cannot know. But the songs do contain the possible interpretation that God intends to redeem his people through the sacrifice of a single individual. The servant songs have been enormously influential in the way the Church has interpreted the death of Jesus. Although they are never referred to explicitly, the details may have influenced the Gospel writers as they told their stories. Luke echoes Second Isaiah when he describes the old man Simeon in the temple prophesying that Jesus would be 'a light for revelation to the Gentiles' (Luke 2:32). Luke also recalls the servant setting his face like flint when he writes that Jesus 'set his face' to go to Jerusalem (Luke 9:51). In Mark's Gospel Jesus says at the Last

Supper that his life will be poured out 'for many' (Mark 14:24). All these phrases carry resonances of phrases of the servant songs. John has Jesus speaking of the Son of Man being 'lifted up' (John 3:14), and drawing all people to himself (John 12:32). It is certainly possible that the figure of the servant, humiliated and then exalted, had an influence on Jesus as he prepared for his death. It is even more likely that this had an influence on the Gospel writers.

What is clear from the Gospels is that none of this occurred to the disciples at the time. They ran away, which was a sensible thing to do. In the everyday religious politics of the time, if the Messiah you followed died it was proof positive that you had backed the wrong man. The movement surrounding a failed Messiah was either wiped out or broke up as quickly as possible. Nobody wanted to voice support for Judas the Galilean when he and his rebel army ended up on crosses, and we have no reason to think that Peter, James and John had any other hope after the death of Jesus than to distance themselves from him and disappear unnoticed. A hint of this attempt is preserved in the story of Peter's denial, which all four Gospels relate (Matthew 26:69 ff; Mark 14:66 ff; Luke 22:54 ff; John 18:15 ff). While Jesus was being questioned in the house of Caiaphas, Peter was lurking around in the courtyard warming himself against the early morning chill by an open brazier. He got into conversation and denied having had anything to do with Jesus. His denial was not all that successful because his Galilean accent marked him out. The fact that this story is in all four Gospels makes it likely to have happened, especially as it paints an unflattering portrait of the leader of the apostles. In the crisis of the kingdom, Peter was not found to be reliable.

Death and burial

Crucifixions could last for days; it was a slow form of death. Jesus actually died relatively quickly. The body of Jesus was taken down from the cross and was buried in a new tomb near the site of the crucifixion. Down the narrow stairway from Golgotha in the church of the Holy Sepulchre is the traditional burial place. The original first-century tomb that Constantine's investigators believed was the authentic tomb of Christ was covered over in the fourth century and turned into a shrine. The current monument dates from the nineteenth century. It is difficult to imagine what the original looked like from the present arrangement in the church, but there are other first-century tombs that have been discovered not far away and that show us what Jesus' tomb must have been like. It was cut out of the rock and sealed with a flat rolling stone, probably a rather bigger one than the small specimen at the Garden Tomb of General Gordon. Jesus' tomb was expensive. It was, apparently, a gift from one of his secret highly placed followers, Joseph of Arimathea (Matthew 27:57–60). Unable to openly support him in his lifetime, he made this last present to his dead Messiah.

Nobody can explain what happened next. The Gospels say that the women who had been present at his death came to visit the tomb of Jesus two days later, after the Sabbath, and found that it was empty. Their initial reaction was terror, which is hardly surprising. They had come out before dawn, hoping to pay their last respects to his body by anointing him with precious spices. In their highly sensitised state they were expecting to give voice to their grief, yet what met them was an inexplicable absence.

The missing body

There have been many attempts to explain what might have happened. One version is that Jesus' followers simply made up the story that the body was missing in order to keep the claim alive that he really was the Messiah. The problem with this theory is that it fails to explain the fact that it was Jesus' women disciples who first witnessed the absence of the body. This was a disaster for the credibility of a false claim since the testimony of a group of women babbling that he was not dead but risen would have counted as evidence *against* any kind of claim that Jesus was alive. Women's evidence was simply not admissible in Jewish law; females had no chance of being regarded as reliable witnesses. According to Luke, they were not even believed by the other disciples (Luke 24:10–11).

Another theory is that the tomb was empty because Jesus never died on the cross at all, and this is what Muslims believe about the death of Jesus. The Qur'an states (Sura 4:156) 'they did not slay him, and they did not crucify him, they had only his likeness. They did not slay him.' There are two ways in which this assertion could be understood. The obvious way is to take it as a claim that a substitute was crucified in place of Jesus, that another human being was somehow persuaded or forced to die in his place. Alternatively, it is a claim that the substitute was a kind of phantom of human or angelic creation. Muslims were not the first to propose this theory. Some early Christians called Gnostics also believed that Jesus had been crucified in appearance only. Neither they nor Muslims could accept that an authentic messenger of God could die a humiliating death. One Muslim sect even teaches that Jesus travelled widely after the crucifixion and eventually died in old age in Kashmir, where a tomb believed to be his is still preserved.

Drugged to survive?

A more plausible possibility is that Jesus was crucified but somehow survived. Later he was rescued from the tomb, severely injured, but alive. If this is what did happen there would have to be an explanation of how Jesus got through the pain of crucifixion. One obvious answer is that he was anaesthetised in some way. People today can live through the injuries of major surgery as long as their capacity to feel pain is deadened. Highly sophisticated anaesthetics have transformed operations and made surgery a much safer and more effective procedure than it has ever been before. But even in Jesus' time there were anaesthetics. One that has been used as an active ingredient until very recently is produced from the mandrake, a plant with purple flowers and a strange forked root. This plant has always been thought to have magical properties. Its narcotic effect was noted by Shakespeare, who has Iago say of Othello, after sowing the suspicion that his wife was unfaithful,

> Nor poppy, nor mandragora [mandrake],
> Nor all the drowsy syrups of the world
> Shall ever medicine thee to that sweet sleep
> Which thou owedst yesterday. (*Othello*, Act 3: Scene 3)

Today, the anaesthetic produced from mandrake can be obtained synthetically, but the properties of this plant were well known in the ancient world. The root was shredded and turned into a solution, which was then used to soak a sponge that was dried and then re-immersed until it was thoroughly saturated with the drug. The sponge would then receive a final soaking in water and the fumes would be inhaled. We know that mandrake was in use at the time of Jesus. Mandrake is a very powerful anaesthetic that not only makes a person unconscious and unaware of pain, but gives an anaesthetised body the appearance of being dead. Breathing is almost undetectable; limbs are paralysed. Could such a drug have been given to Jesus?

The Gospels say that as Jesus was crucified he was offered a sponge soaked with vinegar, but each Gospel describes what was in the vinegar differently. Matthew (27:34) says that it was mingled with gall, Mark (15:23) that it was mingled with myrrh, which was used as a painkiller. Gall here probably just refers to some bitter ingredient, which could have been myrrh. In which case, Matthew was simply making what Mark said clearer. Both accounts say that when Jesus tasted the sponge he refused to drink it. Luke (23:36) says that the soldiers offered him vinegar, but does not say whether Jesus drank it or not. John has a different version. This time, when his death was near, Jesus said, 'I thirst.' A sponge soaked in vinegar was offered to him. He drank and then died. The Gospels are at pains to imply that Jesus did not drink anything that could have relieved his suffering. In John's account the sponge is innocuous. But perhaps the accounts come out this way because it had already been suggested that Jesus had been drugged.

There is certainly a possibility that mandrake or some other strong drug was administered to Jesus, and it is quite likely that the Romans knew about the practice of giving criminals some kind of anaesthetic – and even encouraged it. After all, it was the spectacle of a painful death that really counted, and too much unbearable physical agony on the part of the sufferer could make even hardened onlookers feel uncomfortable. John describes a Roman soldier piercing the side of Jesus after his death (John 19:34). This may well have been to check that he really was dead, not in a drug-induced coma.

So what are the chances that Jesus survived the cross through the use of drugs? The consensus is that they are very slight. The main problem is that it is very difficult to calculate the right amount of mandrake to produce anaesthesia under such extreme conditions of pain without it being irreversible and leading to death. Even today, calculating the exact amount of anaesthetic needed to put a patient to sleep, and then to keep them below the surface of awareness, is not an easy matter. Occasionally, even modern anaesthetic procedures go wrong and patients are harmed or even die. Learning to administer anaesthetics safely is both an exact science and an art that requires years of training and experience. The chances in the first century of getting the right dosage to save Jesus from death while at the same time passing him off as dead were infinitesimal.

Cause of death

The other point at which the drug theory breaks down is when it is confronted with the sheer extent of Jesus' injuries. The usual cause of death in crucifixion was suffocation. The chest muscles weakened under the pressure of gravity caused by the victim's body weight, until eventually he could no longer breathe. Dr Frederick Zugibe believes that Jesus died of a form of acute shock, before suffocation set in. He attributes this to the violent injuries that Jesus had already sustained. There had already been blood loss in the Garden of Gethsemane as Jesus 'sweated blood'. Then he was scourged, most probably with a lash of leather tails with metal weights at the end. These would have torn at the flesh and caused more bleeding. By now he would have been severely dehydrated. The three-quarters-of-a-mile walk to Golgotha would have increased the effects of shock. The Gospels say that he fell, and a stranger had to be enlisted to carry his cross; it is possible that Jesus began to have convulsions. He survived the cross for about six hours while suffering extreme pain in the hands, feet and chest wall. The pain to the nerves in his hands and feet was itself bad enough to put the whole body under severe stress, an agony that even narcotics could not control. Dr Zugibe compares the pain Jesus endured to that of victims of shrapnel wounds in the First World War. Many of them died as a result of the stress to the body of uncontrollable pain.

A third point, which follows on from the last, is that the drug hypothesis offers no explanation of how Jesus recovered from his injuries. It would have taken weeks if not months for him to be able to walk around, travel or hold a normal conversation. In the weeks after his death he would have been an invalid, in need of constant care. Yet the accounts of those who claim to have seen him alive after his death do not suggest that his body was frail or that he was limited by his recent injuries. He was not staggering around in pain, but seemed free to be anywhere.

The final argument against the drug theory is simply that the Romans were professional and expert executioners. There is no reason to think that they made a mistake with Jesus.

Strange appearances

If we cannot escape the conclusion that the real Jesus really did die on the cross, what are we to make of the stories of his resurrection? The Gospels report several occasions on which Jesus appeared to his disciples after his death. There are a number of striking features about these appearances. The first is that they are very varied. Some occur in and around Jerusalem, some back in Galilee. Some happen to named and known members of Jesus' inner circle; some to those disciples who were less close to the centre. All of them reveal Jesus as being in some way *different*. Two disciples walking to Emmaus, a town west of Jerusalem, were joined by a stranger who travelled with them and then, at their invitation, joins them at the inn where they were staying the night. Only when he broke bread for the evening meal did they recognise that it was Jesus (Luke 24:13–27).

What are we to make of these reports? We know from the testimony of countless bereaved people that it is very common for those who have lost loved ones to experience their presence. They hear a voice, see the deceased person in the street, or glimpse a fleeting likeness going up the stairs. These hallucinations seem to come from sudden overwhelming memories that take physical and aural form. There are even stories of people who lost relatives in wartime, and who experienced them returning home unexpectedly, and then disappearing into thin air. Afterwards they discovered that the person had died at the very moment of their appearance. We cannot easily explain such events, but we do know that when there are strong bonds of love between people they can sometimes share thoughts and experiences across great distances. Perhaps the dying person in some way projects an image of themselves that is mysteriously picked up by the one they love? We cannot know. There are cases, of course, where the mind is simply tricked. A stressed, grieving mind can 'see' the one it most desires. The bereaved can hold conversations with those who have died and experience it as a two-way dialogue.

We are bound to ask if the resurrection was the kind of experience that we know can occur in bereavement? Of course, it is possible that some experiences of Jesus after his death could have been of this kind, but it is difficult to make this case for all of them. This is because the appearances of Jesus after the resurrection have an unusual feature that marks them out from the familiar kind of hallucinations. In most cases, the Gospels report that Jesus was not immediately recognised. This is odd –

the whole point of the kind of mind trick that usually happens in bereavement is recognition. The person having the hallucination is overwhelmed by the lost one's presence. They see, they hear, they know. That is what makes these experiences so poignant and so powerful. But the disciples did not experience Jesus like this at all.

Some of the accounts never get to the point of an appearance at all, but remain with the absence of Jesus' body. In Mark's Gospel the women go to the tomb to anoint the body. This was a normal practice before burial, though not so normal *after* burial! However, we can assume that they wanted to say their goodbyes, a natural enough response. On the way they were worried about whether they would be able to get access to the body, ' "Who will roll away the stone for us from the entrance to the tomb?" ' (Mark 16:3). They expect to find the tomb sealed by the usual flat round stone rolled across the entrance; what they actually find is that the stone has already been rolled back. They go into the tomb. Inside, instead of the body of Jesus, they see a young man in white sitting as though he has been waiting for them. He tells them that Jesus is not there, but is risen and gone before them to Galilee where he will meet with them again. The women are to pass this news on to Peter and the other disciples. The reaction of the women is fear and confusion. So scared are they that they say nothing to anyone at all; they simply run away as fast as they can. Mark's account of the resurrection is far from being a triumphant conclusion. So stark and unfinished is his account that his Gospel ends in the middle of a sentence, 'they said nothing to anyone for they were afraid' (Mark 16:6). Or, to be colloquial and to get more of the unfinished feeling of Mark's Greek, 'they said nothing to anyone. They were afraid, you see.'

In other appearances, like the one on the road to Emmaus, the disciples simply fail to recognise Jesus until he does something familiar. It is when he breaks bread that they see who he is. In the most moving and memorable of these stories, Jesus appears to Mary Magdalene in the garden beside the tomb (John 20:1–18). She mistakes him for the gardener and asks him if has moved the body of Jesus. It is only when he calls her by name, 'Mary', that she recognises him.

These stories are not the incoherent accounts of hysterical people. The only version that has an air of real panic and confusion is Mark's. But the rest all differ from one another; no one has tried to tidy up the inconsistencies. Jesus appears in one version to a number of the women, in another version to Mary Magdalene alone. In one account, the women say nothing; in another, they speak but are not believed; in a third, they tell Peter and John who rush to the tomb to find out for themselves. One set of appearances occurs in Galilee, others take place in Jerusalem. What the stories all have in common is that they are beautifully crafted. What is also extraordinary is that the moment of breakthrough when Jesus is recognised is often a moment when a particular memory is being invoked of what Jesus has meant in the life of the person having the experience. The two disciples on the way to Emmaus recognise Jesus as he was at the Last Supper, and perhaps at other communal meals throughout the three years of his preaching career. Mary, one of the outsiders, who was exorcised by Jesus of seven tormenting devils, recognises him when he speaks her name. Perhaps like the mad man from Gadara, Mary, when possessed, had no real sense of who she was. When he exorcised her, Jesus restored Mary's dignity and gave her a sense of worth. When she weeps outside the tomb she is weeping for him and for herself, for all that he had done for her. So it is when he names her that she remembers being restored to herself and recognises Jesus all over again.

The same kind of pattern can be seen in John's version of the appearance to Peter. John's Gospel sets this in Galilee. Peter has apparently returned home with some of the other disciples, and they have resumed their old lives as fishermen. After a fruitless night on the lake they meet a stranger on the shore who impels them to go out again and cast their nets. They do so and take in a large catch. On returning they find that the stranger has lit a fire and is making a breakfast of fish and bread. This is the point at which they recognise Jesus. He is doing what he has done before, making a meal from bread and fish for all to share. Afterwards, Jesus talks with Peter, reminding him of his love for him. The point of this conversation is to undo the wounds of Peter's betrayal. Though Peter has not been faithful to Jesus, Jesus remains faithful to him, and gives him the awesome responsibility of being a shepherd to the new community (John 21:15–17).

It is impossible to assess what historical value these stories have. They are put together with such psychological and spiritual insight that they must be the fruit of years of reflection. They are not so much about the physical resurrection of Jesus, as about the way the disciples continued to experience him as a central presence in their lives and the focus of their deepest loyalty. The stories in the form we have them have been crafted in such a way as to foster belief and loyalty in others; they are part of the Christian gospel. The one thing they do demonstrate to the historian, though, is that the disciples did not permanently lose their faith after Jesus' death. Against all the odds, they regained their faith, becoming convinced that he was indeed risen from the dead. This in itself is an extraordinary phenomenon, given the very final way in which the Jewish and Roman authorities had set about rubbing Jesus out of history.

Unlike other Messiahs, prophets and holy men of the turbulent first century, Jesus simply refused to disappear. We can ask, though, whether there was anything in the Jewish Scriptures that might have given the disciples the idea of resurrection or helped them to interpret their experience of the once dead Jesus in those terms.

According to the Scriptures

The Jews of Jesus' time were familiar with the idea of resurrection. It first occurs in the thirty-seventh chapter of the book of Ezekiel which was written during the exile in Babylon. Ezekiel has a fantastic vision of a valley full of dry, dead bones. These, he is told, are the whole host of the house of Israel. The bones are a metaphor for the exiled people. They are dead, dry, cut off from life, hope and future. In the vision, Ezekiel is told to prophesy to the bones that they will be brought to life. As he speaks there is a rattling sound as the bones begin to move and come together and connect. Then they are covered with muscle and flesh and skin, and finally the whole valley full of the dead rises up. It is a weird, surreal vision, but it has a very straightforward meaning. This is a poetic metaphor for the rebirth of a nation. It is not about corpses reviving or souls surviving death.

Later in Jewish history resurrection does come to apply to people coming to life again after death. In the twelfth chapter of Daniel there is a vision of the end time, a period of final conflict when God's people will be delivered from their enemies. At that point, 'Many of those who sleep in the dust of the earth shall awake, some to everlasting life, and some to shame and everlasting contempt.' This is a kind of communal resurrection in which the wise and the good will be raised to a state where they shine for ever like stars. Although this goes a stage further than Ezekiel, it does not really suggest any kind of active or individual life beyond death.

Jesus used a similar picture of the resurrection in an argument with the Sadducees. The Sadducees did not accept any belief in a life hereafter and they put a case to Jesus to demonstrate, as they saw it, the absurdities of such a belief. They asked Jesus for his opinion of what would happen to a woman who had been married in turn to seven brothers, each of whom died. Eventually, she died too. In the resurrection, they asked, whose wife would she be? Jesus replied that in spite of their apparent orthodoxy, their answer reflected their ignorance of the true meaning of Scripture. When the resurrection happened it would not be a mere continuity of this life. There would be no marriage transactions between those who rise from the dead and no marriages would be recognised, but they 'are like the angels in heaven' (Mark 12:25).

In fact, there is little in the Jewish Scriptures that would have prepared the disciples for the resurrection of a particular individual. Luke says that Jesus explained to the two disciples on the road to Emmaus that it was 'necessary that the Messiah should suffer these things and then enter into his glory' (Luke 24:26). He then describes Jesus 'opening' the Scriptures and interpreting for them the things prophesied about himself. Although the case is being made that the resurrection is all part of the divine plan, the fact that the risen Jesus had to teach the two disciples 'the things about himself' suggests that there was something novel about the resurrection that did not fit neatly into the pattern of promise and fulfilment.

What the disciples probably thought was that Jesus was resurrected as a representative of the whole of God's people. It was not difficult for them to believe that they were in the time of final conflict that Daniel had predicted, for much of Jesus' teaching makes this assumption. From the disciples' point of view, Jesus has endured a martyr's death. He has been a suffering

Messiah. Now, after his death, individuals experienced his presence in a new form. Not as a revived corpse, but as a being from another kind of existence, so strange that they cannot recognise him. The penny begins to drop, and it all begins to click. Jesus' suffering had always been part of the plan; he lived and died according to the Scriptures. Now, he has been resurrected as the first of the righteous of Israel. In spite of all appearances, God's purpose is still on track. The kingdom is on its way.

It is only in the light of this conviction that we can understand the extraordinary transformation of the disciples from runaways into missionaries. Whether they were right to be convinced that Jesus was risen we can only judge for ourselves, but there can be no doubt that they were so convinced. They made a gigantic leap of faith and commitment that altered the course of human history.

Ascension

There are other strands in the Jewish Scriptures that would have helped them interpret how Jesus' death could have turned out to be a part of God's plan. There are examples of particularly holy individuals being taken by God straight into heaven. They have no tombs. Their bodies just vanish. One such was the prophet Elijah who was, apparently, taken up into heaven by a whirlwind (2 Kings 2:11). He was so close to God that he was simply taken straight into his presence. And he was not the first. In the book of Genesis there is another example of one of Adam's descendants, a character called Enoch, who 'walked with God; then he was no more, because God took him' (Genesis 5:24). Other Jewish writings that are not in the Bible elaborate on this theme and describe 'ascensions' of some of the great personalities of the

Jewish Bible, including Abraham, Moses and Isaiah.

The idea of outstanding people ascending to heaven in this way is not unique to Judaism. Greek myths describe heroes ascending into heaven and becoming divine. There are also ancient links between kings and gods. In the ancient world people thought of kings being exalted over their subjects in a way that mirrors the exaltation of gods over human beings. In some societies kings were regarded as divine, as the offspring of gods. Even in ancient Israel the king was regarded as a son of God. The psalms have plenty of parallels between the exaltation of God in heaven and the ascension of the monarch to an earthly throne. In the second psalm God laughs from heaven at his enemies, and declares that he has set his own king on the holy hill of Zion. The king is his son and will receive the nations for his inheritance.

It is not surprising that stories of the ascension of Jesus became part of the early Christian message along with the resurrection. Sometimes the two are seen as quite separate events. Luke says that Jesus appeared to his disciples over a period of forty days. He then describes him being taken up, quite literally, into heaven, disappearing from the eyes of the apostles when a cloud takes him beyond their sight (Luke 24:50-3; Acts 1:9-11). In John's version the resurrection and the ascension go together, and the appearances go on until the end of the Gospel. But Jesus says to Mary Magdalene that she is not to hold on to him physically because 'I am ascending to my Father and your Father, to my God and your God' (John 20:17).

The ascension of Jesus borrows from stories like that of Enoch and Elijah, but it also sets the seal on the belief that he had won through and been vindicated. He is now at the right hand of God in heaven just as he predicted in his confrontation with Caiaphas. As with the empty tomb, we cannot easily judge the historical value of these after-death stories of Jesus, but we can at least see some of the ingredients of Jewish Scripture and belief that went into them and what the first Christians believed they fulfilled. It really was obvious to them that Jesus had fulfilled the Scriptures and was at God's right hand. This was the secret of their astonishing confidence and authority. It was also why the Church came to the conclusion, which it refined over a period of 500 years, that Jesus really was the unique, only-begotten Son of God.

Incarnation

This belief was, and is, extraordinary. The Church came to see Jesus not just as a son of God in the way every good Jew might think of himself. Not the son of God in terms that the great kings of Israel might be regarded as sons of God, because of their anointing and adoption by God. Not even son of God in the sense in which a gifted healer like Hanina ben Dosa might be thought of as being in a special intimate relationship with his heavenly Father. No, Jesus was more than this. He was the unique, only-begotten Son of God, from all eternity. He was God incarnate, God in human form.

This is much more than the New Testament says. The only Gospel that comes near to describing Jesus as God incarnate is that of John. In the first chapter he writes of the eternal word becoming flesh and living among us. That one chapter has had enormous influence on Christian theology, probably more than any other page of the Bible. How did it come to be so important?

The first disciples were not theologians, but they did think something unique had happened because of Jesus. As mono-theists, they believed there could only be one God, and that was Israel's God. They knew, too, that God allowed no images. He could not be visualised and worshipped in the form of a statue or a picture. Yet all through the Scriptures and prayers of Israel there is a longing to see God's face. There was an emotional satisfaction in pagan images that was denied to Jews. Tom Wright thinks that the disciples came to think of Jesus as the visible face of the invisible God. He points out that Jesus had acted with extraordinary authority. He had healed the infirm and the sick and welcomed them into God's kingdom. He had forgiven sinners, which only God could do. He had fulfilled the mission of Judaism to be a light to the nations by reaching out to Gentiles. He stood up to the strong while remaining a man of peace and non-violence. He actually did the things that people prayed to God to do for them.

The Christ of God

When the earliest Jewish Christians prayed to God, they did not begin thinking of Jesus as a second god. They never stopped being monotheists, but it became natural for them to add the name of Jesus, to think of him as being with God, alongside God. This is what the disciple Paul does in his letters when he invokes or gives thanks to God and then adds 'through Jesus Christ'. It is as though it is impossible for those who believe in Jesus to think of God without thinking of Jesus too. Where God is, Jesus is, and so he becomes part of the prayer. The great biblical scholar C. F. D. Moule, who was for many years Lady Margaret Professor of Theology at Cambridge University, used to help his students understand this by saying that Paul thought of Christ as a kind of *atmosphere* in which the early Christians lived and through which everything happened to them.

When the Christian message got out into the Gentile world it met religious pluralism. Gentile converts naturally assumed that

God could take many forms, that the divine was pluriform. It was easier in that context to think of Jesus as a divinity or an angel, a messenger from heavenly realms who had come to earth, preached, healed and conquered evil and then gone back to heaven. Paul taught that the Christ had come among Gentiles who had religious assumptions, which made it easy for them to think of Jesus as a heavenly messenger of this kind.

This is probably why the very earliest writings of the Christian era, those of Paul, show so little interest in the life story of Jesus or in his teachings. Paul preaches a heavenly Saviour, who lived and died and rose again. He preaches Christ as the atmosphere in which Christians live and breathe and pray. Christ, for him, is a cosmic figure who will one day return from heaven to judge the whole world, Jew and Gentile together. It was perhaps because Gentile Christianity so quickly and naturally elevated Christ into a god that the four Gospels came to be written.

Why the Gospels were written

It really was important, twenty or thirty years after Paul, to record the human story of Jesus. That is to say, that he really was born of a human mother and grew up in a named village; that he belonged to a particular family and was brought up an observant Jew; that he brushed against the known political figures of his day; that he called individuals whose names and backgrounds were still known about to be his disciples. If this attempt at a reconstruction is true, then the Gospels, far from being exaggerated and unhistorical, are the first real attempt at disciplined Christian history. They do not spare the embarrassing moments. They tell us Jesus was sometimes harsh and rude. They remind us that he was tempted and knew uncertainty. They show us that he was not in such constant awareness of God that he did not need to pray. They do not spare us from the fact that fear overwhelmed him to the point of breakdown in Gethsemane. Most important of all, they make it impossible for Christianity ever to deny the real humanity of Jesus. He may or may not be the divine figure Christianity claims he is, but he really is human. He is one of us and part of history, which is why it is still possible for historians to investigate his life and for new discoveries to shed further light on who he was and what he believed.

The face of Christ

Therefore we are getting, through historical research, a fuller picture of Jesus than has ever before been possible.

There is one thing we cannot know, which is what Jesus looked like. It sounds so obvious, and yet there is no description of him in the Gospels or anywhere else in the New Testament. Was he short or tall, dark and olive skinned or ruddy faced? (It is unlikely that he was blond!) Did he have straight or curly hair? Brown, blue or grey eyes? Was he fat or thin?

The earliest description of Jesus in words comes from the Church father Origen of Alexandria in the third century. He says that Jesus was short and dark, and rather squat looking, and ugly. This is not at all what we might expect. Origen was almost certainly influenced by the last of the servant songs where Second Isaiah says, 'He had no form or majesty that we should look at him, nothing in his appearance that we should desire him' (Isaiah 53:2).

When the early Christians did start to portray Jesus in stone and paint, about the middle of the third century, they copied the conventions of the art of the time. Thus he appears in cemeteries and tombs as a Roman shepherd, with curly reddish hair and strong arms, wearing a sleeveless tunic. Later Christian artists showed him as a philosopher or teacher, holding up a scroll, surrounded by his disciples – who look like young, eager, Roman students. There are bold attempts to depict Jesus in terms of the religious imagery familiar in the Roman world. One famous portrayal shows him as Apollo, the sun god, with the sun's rays streaming from his head and a chariot with horses beside him. After the conversion of Constantine, the first Christian emperor, Jesus himself begins to appear more like an emperor, enthroned on the world in purple and gold.

Eusebius, the Bishop of Caesarea (AD 260–340), testified that there were images of Christ in his own time that resembled authentic likenesses. He even claimed to have seen one of them. By the sixth century AD sacred pictures were being made of Jesus and the saints that were venerated in worship. By this time, the face of Jesus was taking on the classic form in which we still recognise it today. The classic face of Jesus shows a man in his thirties with long hair parted at the centre, penetrating eyes, straight nose, oval face and beard. The face is traditionally grave, intense and majestic, with a hint of sadness. It is a face everyone instantly recognises because it expresses Christian devotion to Jesus as it developed over the centuries. But it is unlikely to bear much resemblance to the face of the real Jesus.

Can we ever know what he really looked like? All we know for sure is that he was a first-century Galilean Jew, and here the techniques of forensic science may be able to help with this last fascinating quest. Israeli scientists have in their possession literally thousands of skulls and bones unearthed by archaeologists, road builders and even farmers, a proportion of which can be accurately dated to the first century. These human bones are not treated casually or with disrespect; they will all be re-buried once the scientists have finished studying them. These bones may give us the only clue we have as to what Jesus really looked like. What has surprised the scientists is that the typical first-century Jewish skull had a distinctive shape that is quite different from that of modern Europeans, or modern Jews for that matter. The bone structure in the front indicates a very wide face, not the long oval face that Jesus usually has.

Taking a typical skull from first-century Palestine it is possible to reconstruct the kind of face the anonymous possessor of the skull would most probably have had. This has been attempted, and what looks like a real human face emerges. It is a very broad, rectangular face by our standards, with a large hooked nose, a thick neck and a heavy, powerful jaw-line. The forehead slopes forward. The overall look is of a face that we would be more likely to find today in parts of northern Africa.

This is not, of course, the face of Jesus, but it could well be the kind of face that was common in first-century Palestine. It is not a handsome face, but in its reconstructed form it communicates authority, physical strength and intelligence.

Is this anything like the real Jesus? We cannot know. But it does at least show that the golden-haired Jesus of children's Bibles and Hollywood is an invention of our imagination, as is the long-faced Jesus of the Church's tradition. If this recon-structed face were put on the front of Bibles and turned into devotional art, we would not recognise Jesus. We would see a strong and determined man from a non-European world. We would see an intensity around the eyes and the mouth. But what drove him, what he cared about, how he lived and died, we would never be able to guess.

The strength of the figure of Jesus, though, has always been that it contains surprises. Who would ever have thought that a Galilean carpenter would come to be regarded by millions as the human being most like God ever to have walked this planet? So like God, in fact, that he came to be identified with God himself, as the Son of God.

FURTHER READING

Discoveries from the Time of Jesus, Alan Millard (Lion Publishing, 1990).

The Holy Land: An Archaeological Guide from Earliest Times to 1700, Jerome Murphy-O'Connor (Oxford Paperbacks, fourth edition published 1998).

The Oxford Bible Atlas, edited by John May (Oxford University Press Inc., USA, third edition published 1984).

The Oxford Companion to the Bible, edited by Bruce M. Metzger and Michael D. Coogan (Oxford University Press Inc., USA, 1994).